General Theory of Victims

François Laruelle

Translated by Jessie Hock and Alex Dubilet

polity

First published in French as *Théorie générale des victimes* © Mille et une nuits, département de la Librairie Arthème Fayard, 2012

This English edition © Polity Press, 2015

INSTITUT
FRANÇAIS
ROYAUME-UNI

This book is supported by the Institut français (Royaume-Uni) as part of the Burgess programme.

Polity Press
65 Bridge Street
Cambridge CB2 1UR, UK

Polity Press
350 Main Street
Malden, MA 02148, USA

ISBN-13: 978-0-7456-7960-0
ISBN-13: 978-0-7456-7961-7(pb)

A catalogue record for this book is available from the British Library.

Library of Congress Cataloging-in-Publication Data

Laruelle, François.
  [Theorie generale des victimes. English]
  General theory of victims / François Laruelle.
     pages cm
  ISBN 978-0-7456-7960-0 (hardcover : alk. paper) -- ISBN 0-7456-7960-9 (hardcover : alk. paper) -- ISBN 978-0-7456-7961-7 (pbk. : alk. paper) -- ISBN 0-7456-7961-7 (pbk. : alk. paper) 1. Victims. I. Title.
  B2433.L373T4413 2015
  362.8801--dc23

Typeset in 11 on 14 pt Sabon by
Servis Filmsetting Ltd, Stockport, Cheshire
Printed and bound in the UK by CPI Group (UK) Ltd, Croydon CR0 4YY

For further information on Polity, visit our website: politybooks.com

Contents

Translators' Introduction

While translating *General Theory of Victims*, we have made a number of decisions that are decisive for the overall tone and style of the English text. Perhaps the most far-reaching of these concerns the gender of key theoretical terms – victim, intellectual, Man, Man-in-person, human, criminal, philosopher. In French, unlike in English, every word has a grammatical gender. "Victim," for example, is feminine, while "intellectual" is masculine. The problem is intractable because it is two-sided: on the one hand, the text's theoretical positions preclude these terms having any straightforward empirical reference. That is, Laruelle does not seem to intend for us to associate victims with the feminine or intellectuals with the masculine. On the other hand, stripping these terms and their pronouns of grammatical gender would create additional ambiguities in the English text. Although we contemplated using neuters for all of these terms in order to avoid overburdening the English with gendered implications, for the sake of clarity it was imperative to assign these terms distinct genders so that, for example, sentences with frequent pronominal references to both the intellectual and the victim could be parsed.

Because there is no truly elegant solution, we decided on a pragmatic one, which, furthermore, we believe at least partially reflects the theoretical orientation of Laruelle's argument. In our translation, several of these terms – Man, intellectual, criminal, and philosopher – take masculine pronouns. Generally speaking, these terms refer to figures or functions "in the world." In contrast, we render the terms that are more specific to Laruelle's own lexicon – victim, Man-in-person – as neuter. Generally speaking, these terms refer to what Laruelle calls "generic" figures. This is by no means a perfect solution, particularly because many of these terms function in the text variously as "generic" *or* "in the world" (e.g. "Man" refers sometimes to a philosophical or worldly conception and, at others, to a generic figure equivalent to Man-in-person). It seemed to us that changing a single term's gender depending on context would be unnecessarily confusing; furthermore, doing so would have forced us to make theoretical decisions that are best left to the reader's interpretation.

In making some terms neuter, we do not want to suggest that the victim or Man-in-person necessarily lack gender, but rather that their gender is radically underdetermined. Given that Laruelle argues that a general theory of victims cannot assume that the object designated by the term "victim" is known, the indeterminacy of the neuter seemed appropriate, reminding readers that there is no easy designation for the victim and thus preventing a false sense of concreteness. We chose the masculine pronoun for the terms Man, intellectual, criminal, and philosopher in order to hew to the French, and also because at least one of these terms – Man – is obviously gendered, even in English. On the other hand, although we considered using the feminine pronoun for the victim in order to avoid any masculinist tendencies, we did not because such a gesture would, inversely, overdetermine Laruelle's argument which does not emphasize the gendering of victims. It seemed important not to imply that the text theorizes the gendering of victims as feminine when in fact it does not.

Another decision was how to translate the term *vécu*, which Laruelle uses frequently. We have rendered its adjectival forms as "lived" and its substantive forms as "lived experience." We would like to warn readers that, although the term is directly connected to the German *Erlebnis*, Laruelle's use of the term no longer carries a strong association with consciousness or subjective experience. Indeed, in a number of places even the substantive form of the term could have been rendered more directly and simply as "the lived," but we opted for consistency over elegance in this instance. Out of the same concern for consistency, we rendered *vécu-sans-vie* as "lived-experience-without-life."

Several singular phrases might give the reader pause. Laruelle coins a number of concepts in this text. We have chosen to render the unusual French expression *une fois chaque fois* as "once each time" in order to stress the contemporaneity of the occurrence described. For his term *avant-priorité*, we have followed accepted translation in using "prior-priority," whereas for *avant-premier(e)*, we have chosen "prior-to-the-first." Although this translation is a bit cumbersome, it nevertheless has the benefit of retaining the echo with *avant-priorité*.

Another term with a particular usage is *ressuscité*; as an adjective, as in *la victime ressuscité*; as a substantive, as in a phrase like *la futuralité des Ressuscités*; or as part of a new term, as in a phrase like *le Ressuscité-en-personne*. We have rendered it as "arisen" throughout. Thus, we have rendered the first case as "the arisen victim," the second as "the futurality of the Arisen," and the third as "the Arisen-in-person." This decision is justified by the fact that the term is mutated from a Christian context, something to which the text itself attests. Rendering it as "arisen" has allowed us to capture these echoes throughout.

Several other terminological choices should be kept in mind. The English "mankind" serves throughout the text as a rendering of the French *genre humain*. This is a standard translation, but one that obscures the multiple resonances of the French term, which could also be translated as "human species," "human genre," or "human sort," associations that should be kept in mind because they are reactivated in the text.

For the purpose of conceptual consistency, we have rendered the word *suffisance* throughout as "sufficiency," but we hope the reader will keep in mind that in French the word also has a touch of arrogance to it, meaning at times self-sufficiency and even self-importance. Similarly multivalent is the French *force*, which in English could be translated as either "force" or "strength." Instead of alternating between the two English translations, something which might mislead the reader as to the consistency of Laruelle's vocabulary and the emphasis of his meaning (especially in chapter 3 where the word is particularly frequent and important), we have rendered it as "force" throughout. This is in keeping with previous translations, which have also emphasized "force." Common practice guided us in translating *de-dernière-instance* – "of-the-last-instance." This is the established translation, but we hope that readers will keep in mind the other French meaning of *instance*, which is "authority." We decided to render the peculiar verb *sous-venir* as "coming-under," but the reader should also keep in mind that it evokes the French word for memory, *souvenir*.

As is well known to readers of Deleuze and Guattari, the French term *plan* has the dual meaning of "plane" and "plan." We have generally rendered it as "plane," except for the few times where "plan" made more idiomatic sense in English (as for example in the reference to *le plan du salut* which we rendered as a "plan of salvation"). Throughout, *vaincu* is rendered as "defeated," as in "the defeated" for *les vaincus*. Finally, we have decided to follow the tradition of translations of Althusser in rendering the French *conjoncture* directly as "conjuncture." Meanwhile, we decided to render the French *dispositif* the few times it occurs in the text as "arrangement."

Lastly, but most importantly, we would like to thank all those who encouraged and helped us to translate this text. Particular thanks are due to Daniel Hoffmann, to whose elegant French we owe any touch of class in our English translation, Catherine Talley, whose excellent advice always kept us grounded, and Rocco Gangle, for reading the nearly finished manuscript. This translation would not be possible without the support of two people in particular: Anthony Paul Smith, whose offhand but sincere suggestion over dinner in Liverpool that we translate *General Theory of Victims* set this whole project in motion. From the outset, Anthony's generosity and insight have proven invaluable. The second, of course, is François Laruelle himself, whose enthusiasm, encouragement, and guidance throughout the process of translation have been indispensable.

Preface

Philosophy has never been that blurry thought riddled with exceptions that it is for intellectuals successful in the media. Without being a science in the strict sense of the term, philosophy shares several of science's requirements and cannot, precisely for that reason, be content with empirical material, historical facts, narratives and images, or testimony. All of this gives too easy an idea of the concrete. In particular, a problem like that of victims is a challenge; it paradoxically demands to be given a theoretical space, a problematic sufficiently closed to limit the indetermination of utterances made, sufficiently open to permit conceptual invention. This is why the body of this research, the Introduction included, is framed by two texts. The first, "Theoretical preparation and precaution," sets the coordinates for a relatively rigorous space and the vocabulary of its object and of its method. Without making it essential reading and without saying "Let no one enter here who does not cross this portal," that is, the portal of several "non-standard" philosophical notions, it greatly facilitates entry into the depths of the philosophical cave containing the mass graves of victims. We will enter it armed with elementary quantum notions. The second is a "Restatement of the overall argument," which presents the argument in a condensed form. The entirety of the argument is an ethics for the philosophers, professional or not, that we aspire to become, without knowing that we all already are philosophers spontaneously, and, from our point of view, still all too innocently.

Elements of this essay were presented as a lecture at the International College of Tunis at the invitation of Ms Hélé Beji, with an introduction by Philippe Petit.

Theoretical preparation and precaution

In order to ensure its rigor and efficacy, a general theory of victims must expunge many useful or asserted nuances and organize itself around several fundamental concepts. Moreover, it is impossible for such a theory to speak of victims "in themselves" the way common sense, the media, and thus philosophy speak of them, assuming that this object, its production, its affects, and its tasks are all well known. We do not know [*savons*] what a victim is. We know [*connaissons*] nothing of it but symptoms, and we must organize ourselves in order to produce its concept with the two means at our disposal, which enlist a philosophy we will call "non-standard."

The problems are treated according to an orientation known as generic and a method that borrows from quantum theory or, through its extension to the problems of the human sciences, "quantum-oriented" theory. This is a somewhat novel combination and one that, above all, has an important displacement effect: it passes from philosophy and its morals to a formal and more elevated plane, an ethical plane centered on relations, this time between man as a generic being and all of philosophy as a purveyor of morals. The generic orientation will leave the last humanists unsatisfied because humans are here defined as Man-in-person or without humanism, only partially axiomatizable by philosophy or with its help. The second orientation will frustrate physicists, who will wonder what they have to do with and for victims. These two difficulties, "superposed" by a procedure from quantum physics, will define a non-standard theory for humans as victims and for the ethics they demand. For us, the moral and the ethical are distinguished from one another as philosophy and non-standard thought.

The generic orientation, human but not humanist or philosophical, is centered on the notions of "Man-in-person" and "Victim-in-person," notions meant to avoid the classic definitions of man such as "rational animal," "political animal," "metaphysical animal," and so on. The generic is a process of the reduction of any given philosophical or macroscopic entity, of its nature as doublet, double, or double transcendence (consciousness, ego, or a psychosociological identity). It is a reduction to a phenomenal immanence, lived but objective, subjected to the quantum principle of superposition, *which is not a principle of logical identity*. It settles case by case, which is to say once each time, the phenomena of an undulatory or vectorial order, which are linear despite their interference. Nevertheless, such phenomena, which can be added without metaphysical identity, can be paradoxically called "in-person."

In-person defines the One rather than Being. But which One? The One as the real, no doubt, but such a question straightaway falsifies the problem by specularly projecting the answer. One-in-One is already a more precise answer. We will say that in-person is said of the in-One no less than of the appearance of the in-One, of the unique, once-each-time face of the in-One, which has no doublet, does not look at itself in the mirror, and has only this uniface. Under these conditions, in-person always specifies the human or its extensions as generic rather than Being or being [*l'être ou l'étant*]. It results neither from an analytical inclusion nor a synthetic addition of a second term to the first. The superposition that produces it is a "specific" operation and a "specific" real, which owe nothing to logico-philosophical identity, a transcendental one for example, and concerns only what we call the One and not Being. But the in-person becomes amphibological if we relate it back to the massive, in-itself distinctions of philosophy, for example of being and appearing, or of the I and the other, of the I and the stranger. If we persist in referring the in-person back to these coordinates of philosophical space, it receives a double aspect, at once ontological and phenomenological, and thus amphibological. However, if it is said of the human real as One rather than as Being, it is also said of its appearance, except that this appearance is no longer the appearance of Being but of the One; it is the phenomenon of the Stranger, the unique face of the One-without-unity. Just as the One as radical immanence or the One-in-One is substituted for Being, a phenomenology of the One is substituted for a phenomenology of Being.

As for the quantum-oriented procedure for the

treatment of humans, it calls on a matrix of organization through a superposition of opposing givens, dialectical or not, treated as variables, and in the end, as vectors. It indexes their products to the benchmark of an immanence structured algebraically, as quantum theory is prone to do (the imaginary or complex number). The in-person of the One or of humans is thus obtained by a method that associates a non-dialectical conjugation of opposites or philosophical planes as formalized variables – Being and Appearing, the I and the Stranger – with, on the other hand, the algebraic interpretation that transforms them into lived phenomena that are at once undulatory and particulate, which is to say, into vectors. The result is a simplification of doublets and a weakening of philosophical power.

This generic simplification or reduction is neither simply excessive, nor simply subtractive. As "imaginary" in the algebraic sense, it has something excessive in relation to the state of a given thing, but it is less excessive than the always-double philosophical transcendence. In a way, it is a withdrawal or a moderate (radical) subtraction in relation to philosophical transcending, which is absolutely excessive, to the point of reaching "platonic ravings" (Kant). It is subtraction as a solely radical excess, one that asserts the core of "weak force" of humans (and of victims), and also of the concepts dedicated to them. However, the generic and "quantum-oriented method" does not stop at this operation. Opposites (being and appearing, Being and being, nature and culture, etc.) have not vanished completely; they and their (macroscopic) relations reappear in the flowing course of superpositions, this time as phenomena no longer undulatory but particulate, or, all too briefly, microscopic. It is obvious that the superposition of being and appearing, or even, as we will explain, of criminal and victim, of persecutor and persecuted, strictly speaking has no empirical sense or logical identity, and must open up the way towards an admittedly "material" or lived formalism and an ethics for philosophy rather than towards the description of a state of a thing. These superpositions have no empirical sense until the opposing instances are given, recorded, and secured as distinct. And yet, they are no longer superpositions of states in the rigorous sense of the term, which only applies to undulatory phenomena. They are nothing but simple identifications, which are more or less exact collections of transcendent terms incapable of creating a true immanence. Doubtless, the criminal and the victim must have points in common that quickly become points of disjunction, like interferences and intermediary states, but they are not superposed in a quantum sense. So that they can be superposed, the "genre" of objects or of matter, the genre of reality, must be changed in order to enact less a *metabasis allo genos* than a passage to the genre of the real par excellence, which is "mankind" [*genre humain*], to which superposition applies. In shifting phases and under distinct reasons, Man-in-person is the condition under which philosophy and its ethics are placed.

Under the stratum of political, racial, catastrophic, and humanitarian determinations – everything that makes up contemporary victimology as theory of any victim whatsoever upon which the media feeds – the destiny of victims takes another form at once more complex and more intelligible than in its phenomenological and existential treatment. Engaged here under a non-victimary and no longer victimological guise is man in his entirety as a relation of quantum, and not only phenomenological, complementarity with the world, as a generic subject and not only as existence (*Dasein*). It is a question of transferring the existential conception of the victim without denying it – it is an invariable given of its problem – to a more rigorous and scientific discipline, and of establishing victims in the rightful place they demand.

In philosophical, ontological, and phenomenological planning, victimology and criminology, vengeance and justice, and so on, are distinct and remain so; they are preserved as separate determinations (from whence their "sublation," *Aufhebung*). Under the eruption of the mathematical Idea, philosophy imagines, for example, crossings or vertical becomings between planes, "eruptions" of being in appearing, and inverse retroactions, an ontico-ontological difference (Heidegger), whether transcendental or topological by torsion. It is definitively a hierarchical thought despite efforts here and there to nuance and attenuate this imperious character. By contrast, in superposition, be it undulatory or particulate, determinations are interlaced and unlocalizable; there are phases rather than planes. Must we decide in favor of a chaos of the type "we are all criminals, all victims," in favor of the absence of order, under the pretext that hierarchy is broken into a thousand pieces – pieces that still make the world but no longer make mankind? Superposition and intrication, which are the life, or rather the lived experience, of mankind, establish a new order on the ruins of hierarchy: the order-without-hierarchy of mankind as prior-to-the-first insurrection, and not as first over individuals and their diverse groupings.

Man-in-person is not commutative with the human subjects that partake of it; this is the root of justice.

But where does this distinction – of the first in the philosophical sense and the Prior-to-the-first or even the Last Instance, which troubles or subverts the priority of philosophy – come from, and how is this distinction not a vestige of hierarchy? Let us return to the generic matrix, which lays out a lived materiality of superpositions and intrications of variables conceptual in origin and taken from philosophical morals. How does this matrix function on the whole? We said that the variables or properties of this "object" that is Man-in-person are indexed to an imaginary number of the sort mobilized by quantum theory. It implies a subtraction in excess – the excess of immanence – in relation to the in-itself reality of mathematical or philosophical concepts. Why? The terms called opposite are not simply "philosophical"; rigorously analyzed, they are doubled, because philosophy is never simple but always returns a second time to the scene of the crime. This is an illusion that allows philosophy to survive: to be thought simple in the form of terms called "philosophical," whereas philosophy takes care always to return a second time and to reassure or reaffirm itself. But now, with the matrix, it is possible to index the opposites and their products not only to philosophy but also to a science, quantum theory, which also makes a "return" or, precisely, "turns" (Heidegger, but in a quantum rather than an ontological sense) in an undulatory form or by a superposition that is irreducible to the return repeatedly trotted out by philosophy. This interpretation of the matrix through the quantum indexing of relations between opposite terms is, if we hold to it, the inverse and the symmetrical of its philosophical interpretation. But what interests us is its effect, which is neither reducible to a simple inversion nor to a symmetry of effects. The quantum interpretation of the matrix, which will have it be constituted uniquely of superpositions and intrications, has the effect of under-determining the philosophical terms and relations as particulate, that is to say, now as simple and no longer double transcendences, as "particles" algebraically reduced to the *quarter* of conceptual corpuscles. It is a debasing, decline, or clinamen of theological and philosophical transcendences for the benefit of mankind, whose weak force of ascension, insurrection, even "resurrection" is thus affirmed and justified. If there is a radical argument against racism, it is this: *mankind is indeterminate*.

The final consequence of our ethical problem: Is the balance of justice in equilibrium? Equilibrium is an appearance that fulfills as much as possible the victims' natural need for vengeance, using the tribunal to settle their scores and obtain reparation, proceeding with the juridical and philosophical means that renew the "macroscopic" harassment of victims. In the generic real of humans, the concept of which is obtained as indeterminate or probable, there is no equilibrium of this sort, which is ultimately quantitative despite the impossibility of a completely accountable settlement. Equilibrium is obtained qualitatively in a heterogeneous and intricated way, by debasing the sufficiency (the doublets) of philosophical or victimological means. This debasement, this decline of institutional justice, is the effect of the prior-priority of mankind and thus of victims-in-person. A complete conceptual reorganization of the concepts of justice is necessary to definitively escape the circle of vengeance produced by intervening tribunals and their mediation. The Victim-in-person or generic Victim, and not the individual (that is, social and institutional) victim, is the mediate-without-mediation, the under-determining condition of justice, that is, of the juridical and philosophical relations between victim and criminal. The paradox is that, to eradicate so natural a vengeance, justice must no more be entrusted to the institution than to individual victims. So to whom? To victims taken as a generic body; but this is only the condition of justice, not its subject or its object. From this comes the ethical precaution that extends the theoretical one: Justice is a utopia or a philo-fiction, which has only as much of a future as Man-in-person itself.

Introduction

The intellectual and "his" victim

The victim belongs to the new politico-quotidian doxa. The less people take the trouble to disclose its phenomenon, which remains hidden or all too exposed, the more effusive it becomes. The victim's overrepresentation is the forgetting of its origin, its necessity, and its contingency. Like any term that sees its media moment arrive, the victim passes through a stage of expansion and then of nausea, of ascendance, and of decline. By the time we grasp it, it is already perhaps too late; it is theoretically dubious, eroded by the media and buoyed by the securitarian and juridical rise of crime. As though it were miming and fabricating an artificial unconscious, media corruption has made the victim a new ethical value, a point of condensation and effervescence, of the exacerbation of ideological conflicts. Hence there are affects proper to the excess of information, like the nausea that affects certain philosophers.

It was the previous century that gave a human figure

---

to the victim and to evil, stripping them of their ontological and theological rags. Now, the victim is the
phenomenon that renders the experience of evil accessible to us. If not for flashes from literature, the poets,
and the Gnostics, "high" philosophy (Kant aside) will
have been a bracketing of the problem of victims,
and along with it, after a fashion, the problem of evil,
occluded by theodicy and confused with "original
sin." For good reason, only Jewish thinkers have dealt
with this problem. Philosophers developed a strategy
of "looking away" (Nietzsche) from evil and death,
practicing a sidelong view. Some today are more casual,
practicing an imperial forgetfulness and a tabula rasa
in the name of eternal truths. Evil comes once more to
mind in the specific form of "crime against humanity"
(and soon of crime against animality?), and henceforth
forms a conjuncture: "human rights," "victim rights,"
and psychology are proposed as somewhat vicious ad
hoc explanations that form a universal and dispersed
"victimologism."

If a theory of victims does not yet exist explicitly as
such in philosophy, it is because philosophy is more
interested in force, power, and domination, primar-
ily its own. For philosophy, the victim is a secondary
object to which it retains but a few allusions. Ancient
philosophy was only aware of it in the anonymous form
of the victim of destiny, maliciousness, and vengeance.
The classical period, more interested in war, made
the victim into inevitable collateral damage, bringing
forth the lamentation of poets and a first intellectual
defense (Voltaire is an example, but not the only one).
The philosophy of the twentieth century, following the
two world wars and the programmatic and systematic

ideological and ethnic exterminations that accompanied them, extended the concept of the victim and its causes and dramatized it, but always laterally, marginally, as an exception to the proper philosophical order. The victim had to pass a quantitative threshold – that of a "great number" – and persecution an ethnic and technological threshold for it to finally become interesting and visible, for its concept to spread juridically and through the media [*médiatiquement*]. Gradually, it became an object "of testimony," privileged by intellectuals who took up its defense, but also in the media, which actualized and bore witness to it, drawing it from its meager existence and invisibility. The victim is now a blurred, ambiguous generality, an object of indiscriminate use. Forgotten by conceptual thought, it is now overexploited by images and information in the doxa of "we are all victims." Hence, the "anti-victimary" reaction of some and a new call for "strong thought."

Our goal is different: to relocate the victim, if possible, from the phase of being an intellectual and media object to the status of an object of knowledge, from its image to its concept. If the victim was "forgotten" by institutional and official philosophy and led astray by compassionate voyeurism, we maintain that it was just as poorly defended by the "talkative mutes" (Augustine), the intellectuals devoted to its cause.

This essay formalizes the relationship of intellectuals to victims as regards their final touchstone or "last honor." It is above all a question of those contemporary intellectuals who in general have lost their Marxist points of reference and shamelessly surrendered to liberalism. It must be said that they occupy an intermediary region, subject to fluctuations between instances or orders of thought. Since here it is not simply a matter of "intellectual" conflict, we will not name names, except for the paradigmatic ones. They are polarized by two attractors, which sketch an indistinct, shabby space where the squabbles of power lead to its dungeons. The first is the established power, whatever it is, because intellectuals revolve around it, now closer, now farther away, always with the indecency of a weather vane. Their second center of gravity is precisely the victim. Our thesis is that philosophy, for which they are the emissaries, rushing to derive a profit without the work it requires, does not permit them to escape the vicious circle, through which it shakes them like puppets, swinging them between powers and victims in a reversible, alternating manner.

Our problem is how to escape this duality of vicious motivations. We, too, sketch a duality, but a displaced one: it is no longer made up of motivational poles, but of two possible figures of intellectuals, defined by the respective uses they make of these motivations: the "media intellectual in the broad sense," who is engaged or embedded by power and who emerges through the press and the media and derives profit from this, is content to represent victims, to photograph them in language, writing, or image. But to this portrait, already sketched a thousand times by others, we add another supplementary trait: he is embedded in and by philosophy, coming from it and tending towards it, recognizing explicitly, and often also implicitly, its authority first or last. This poor use of philosophical means is his weakness: he is a philosophizing intellectual. And then, there is the "generic" or "under condition" intellectual, who labors under the under-determining but in-the-last-instance condition, but this time the victim's rather than philosophy's. He, too, has dealings with power, but only insofar as he knows that even the worst are legitimizable (and not only legitimated) by philosophy. He does not allow himself to be completely manipulated by philosophy, which he learns to put to good use.

We examine different aspects of the philosophizing intellectual: his theoretical strategy, his malaise and his treason, his victimological pathos, but also victimization as a process of redoubled or multiplied pain inflicted upon the victim. On the side of the generic intellectual, we examine the notions of "weak force" and "strong force," of "survivor" and "arisen," and we attempt to pose the most difficult problem, that of the reasons for persecution and extermination (why do we kill?) and their indexation to generic man rather than to a religious or ethnic scale. It is a question of founding ethics on the unlocalizable and sometimes unidentifiable victim rather than on the metaphysical or philosophical force that took him for profit or loss. This would follow a movement of thought begun, for example, by Levinas (*Humanism of the Other*), and would better agree with our experience of the past century and draw out its consequences.

The ethics stemming from philosophy is a surviving ethics without any great effect or relevance. It is ideologically dominant, theoretically vicious, and makes man into one of its "functions" or "objects." For us, it is rather a question of elaborating, in a "messianic" margin of philosophy, with philosophy's help but without its authority, an ethics of defense of mankind in every one of its possible figures.

All of this assumes another idea of man than that

of Greek metaphysics, where man is organized by the transcendence of the cosmos or even that of Judaic metaphysics, where he is subordinated to the infinite transcendence of God. We call it "generic" in order to suggest that it is restricted to mankind alone, as well as to suggest its simplified, reduced, and neutralized sub-philosophical constitution. Thus, a different idea of the generic intellectual and his tasks, which are no longer classically heroic (virtue, happiness, courage) or heroico-political (taking sides against the powers that be, defense of democracy, etc.), but in prior-priority the defense of victims.

We pursue a more rigorous and more "human" theory than philosophy usually pursues, devoted as it is to the cosmos and to being, to the sciences and to the gods. A certain theoretical practice is capable of itself being the "compassion" philosophy scarcely shows. The highest thought boasts of its proud virtues while mocking weak passions – Spinoza sadness, Hegel the "beautiful soul," Nietzsche pity – to the point of having rendered these affects unbearable and repulsive. Against philosophy's sufficiency, we introduce into philosophy a Principle of Compassion, which will substitute itself for pity, and likewise for vengeance and heroism. This will be the way, for us as well, to militate within theory and not necessarily outside of it, as in the classical "humanitarian" project, and within philosophy itself with the aim of transforming the victimological aporias. In lieu of hiding in ethnic, political, moral, or cultural generalities, which destroy the human intelligibility of phenomena and their type of universality, let us pose the problem of intellectual assistance to victims on other grounds. Victims ought to be ethically assisted by "non-philosophical" rather than ontological thought. This assistance is the function of intellectuals, in their old and, above all, new definition. The first task is paradoxical: thinking humanity as indivisible by cultures, communities, and races, while at the same time as not being a transcendent unity like essence or nature. An indivisible that is not a unity or an essence, ethics will formulate this as philosophically indefinable but axiomatically operable. The only solution that still seems possible to us is to make man the "object" of an axiom or a system of axioms emptied of philosophical determinations, but an axiom of which man would at the same time be the "subject," or more precisely, the lived or neutralized materiality, what we call an *"oraxiom"* (a generic portmanteau word for the superposition of the oracle and the axiom, or the axiom-subject).

If humans in their non-sufficiency cannot individually fight against worldly harassment and historical persecution, if they need an intellectual subject to assist them with this operation, and as persecution in any case implies this subject, it is ultimately in that which we call "Man-in-person" that salvation is to be found and, in the same gesture, that the radical cause of its victimization will be actively denounced. *Man is the only animal capable of being persecuted as such but also capable of insurrection without divine aid.* These oraxioms are too weighty to be explained for now. Because they do justice to victims and can determine an ethics for philosophy, we prefer them to the vicious definition of the rational animal, which sacrifices them once and for all. Having voided all messages, universal communication reduces kerygma and promise to contractual exchange, and philosophy itself to a speculative activity of "derivatives."

In the middle of this debris, we are left with two types of instruments: the form-vector [*forme-vecteur*] of algebra on the one hand, and the lived-form [*forme-vécue*] of axioms on the other. We must continue to "make do" with this material, poor as it is.

We assemble this research under the generic name of *Victim-in-person*, an ethical modality of Man-in-person. *It is the victim insofar as it determines in-the-last-instance the representation and transformation of the defense work done by intellectuals.* It is not a particular or individual victim, but the state of humans insofar as they are capable as such of being persecuted, victimizable de jure but not always explicitly victimized de facto. The victim is not victim immediately, but is immediately capable of being or of becoming victim. The victim is the most exposed depth of humans, their capacity to be *defeated* on occasions that also revive this capacity *as a weak force of resistance.* The victim feels itself a victim (rather than nothing, because it is always in correlation with the world), but does not yet understand itself as such; the victim has the immanent knowledge proper to the defeated, but must actualize it in an understanding and a Principle of Compassion, which runs between victims and which intellectuals in the broad sense must assume. There is no absolute and in-itself victim; the victim is caught in a process of continual victimization, victim also of not yet knowing who and what its executioner is. The victim is defined by a radical passivity, not an absolute one such as Levinas attributes to the I. Radical passivity is that which cannot, by definition, react with an excess of power or an over-power. It is impossible for it to react as a reflex, but it is capable of acting totally otherwise, by the de-potentialization of philosophical over-power. Only the victim is capable, in-the-last-instance and with the involuntary assistance of its murderer, who helps the victim actualize its knowledge-of-being-victim, of safeguarding its human dignity in all cases: the victim has the final resources to do this. Indeed, the identity of the victim, if it must be defined physically or generically, is of a special nature, which appeals to proto-quantum procedures of super-position or interference and not at all to psychological or social identification. Additionally, we will say that the identity of the victim is a reprise and not a repetition. The identity of the executioner is of a wholly different nature, pertaining to the philosophical transcendence of history or of the world, and partaking of repetition. But it never victimizes an individual without actualizing its knowledge-of-being-victim and thus the resistance proper to the defeated.

A relatively rigorous theory of the victim must outstrip the discourse of power and domination characteristic of every philosophy, inducing its debasement or decline. It presumes that the victim is less its object than its condition *prior-to-the-first or in-the-last-instance* (which amounts to the same thing), transforming victimology shot through with philosophy. Placing all philosophy, whether victimary or anti-victimary, under this condition implies that the hesitations and vicious circles of contemporary victimology, however practically useful they may be, will be nothing more than symptomatic material for a rather more upright theory determined by a last criterion or an "ultimate honor," that of a thought oriented or under-determined by the victim. Put another way, in order to summarize this undertaking in a few words, it is necessary to remove ethics from philosophy, which is nothing but one of its materials, and place ethics under the condition of the Victim-in-person. This axiom distributes its effects in three more specific statements: (1) the Victim-in-person is the sole object of ethics; (2) ethics is not, or is no longer, a sector of philosophy, but its usage under condition; (3) even philosophy called ethical is nothing but a means of ethics-according-to-the-victim.

At first glance, the reader may find that this essay indulges in a rather morbid and humanist taste for victims. Moreover, the poverty of philosophical vocabulary, scant and stereotypical as it is, constrains us to awaken, for example, "man" and "compassion," to retrieve them from their recent deaths, whatever the cost and however much we may be threatened by the spectral existence of humanism. One might think that we are refusing to open the mass graves of history to the great sun of Reason, the mass graves that give Reason its profundity or perhaps, who knows, create the depths of God's inhumanity, like eternal truths create the depths of divine understanding. One might think that we are closing them up too quickly, just as someone, fascinated or stunned, closes off a dreadful sight or memory upon its secret. It would have no doubt required a Christ to command that Lazarus rise up and come out of his "sickness unto death" (Kierkegaard). All hope for a "resurrection," or at least for a new understanding of it, will not be lost. Now that the old divine plan for salvation is no more than a memory of which only a trace remains, now that the victims of history into which it was transformed bear witness in some sense to a traceability, and now that this is the sole, final message left to us, a question remains to be asked: *Who still deserves to arise?* Our response is without a doubt very intuitive but can be set out with means other than exclusively philosophical ones. *Only victims, that is, humans in-prior-priority, deserve to arise and are likely able to do so.*

The Victim-in-Person

The axiom of man as victim

Our ethics is based on a theology of the Good and the hierarchy it forms with Evil. Exhausted, deconstructed, driven to extremes by the clashes of history and the variations of philosophy combined, it is a survivor ethics for Survivors, who have shaken off all norms and hopes and are backed into their entrenchments, be it a relativist ideology of the limit and forced retreat, or an apology for a purifying terror, or even a chaos of "human" considerations. We intend to draw out the final consequences of this situation. Our conjuncture has two features. In the first place, the heritage of a century that was quantitatively more criminal than others (now a technological possibility), inscribing it in the depths of consciousness and in the mass graves of memory. But of this century it will surely be said that it legitimated crime with all the rationales of culture and with philosophy's congenital impotence, which warrants philosophy's resignation, and a hijacking of its mission, who knows?

Then, an excess of means could just as well be the means of criminality as those of justice or defense. Obviously, it is possible to take up the "modern" defense of this century against its "renegade" denigrators and to celebrate its "passion for the real"; the only problem is that, as is customary with philosophy, we are dealing with the operation of self-defense and denial. More serious than the collapse of humanism with feet of clay is the immense philosophical self-justification and the denial of its participation in evil. We are not drawing a contrast between the great lost figure of Man and the small differences of contemporary nano-humanism, nor do we attempt to bring it back once more and put it back on stage and back in the saddle. It will certainly be a question of "humans," but in an expanded and focused concept, the "Humans-in-person," and under their figure the "Victim-in-person," both of which are generic rather than philosophical symbols.

If man disappeared with humanism, it is foolish to want to go backwards by reforming the same concepts, reformulating a new humanism under the same conditions as the old, that of a "homodicy" crowned by a theodicy or a justice of the Good. To give a certain right to the reality of evil, let us introduce it into the concept of man. But in what form? Not that of the criminal – that would be too easy – but that of the victim as the non-good that the Good needs, in the same way Being needs non-being to exercise all of its possibilities. We are not going to declare in frustration that man is inherently an evil and criminal being, a new version of sin, but rather that he is at least a victim, the recipient, bearer, and displayer of evil. This is certainly not the same thing as the front and back of a two-faced being, even though the two sides are linked and man can thus appear as Janus-faced, because that would yield to an overly simple unitary and dialectical causality. To want to define man by the predicates of Good or Goodness, to place ethics directly in man's essence, and to be surprised by history's ironic and cruel refutations is to expose oneself to a vicious circle. Our thesis is that man is "fundamentally" a victim or an "object" of evil, and occasionally a criminal, that it belongs to his essence to be virtually a victim, and that his criminal effectiveness is contingent and cannot be used to define him. It is a question of getting rid of the duality of Good and Evil that holds man in its forceps. He belongs to the sphere of evil rather than to the non-human world only by virtue of being a victim, the addressee of persecution – this is the non-active but nonetheless real manner of participating in evil without doing it, by submitting to it par excellence. This is not an obvious thesis for philosophy. It is of course not a question of simply inverting the hierarchy of Good and Evil, but of inverting it in the name of this non-acting, the real, which predisposes man to victim status, and of putting evil in prior-priority instead of in priority. We will not say that humans are passive and allow themselves to be defeated by complicity, because it is in the non-acting of the victim that the resistance to the criminal is manifested, and from this resistance the act and the very person of the criminal are deduced. For its part, resistance to evil is no longer the occurrence of a native and immediate goodness. In-prior-priority of Good and Evil as transcendentals of philosophy, there is a generic non-acting, or passivity, and resistance, which come from further away than from these transcendental characters.

One of the means for extracting the problem of man from its humanistic, and furthermore, philosophical, rut is to consider that man's real potency [*sa teneur en réel*] expresses itself in his victim status, in particular through the expanded concept of "crime against humanity" which distills his entire problem. Furthermore, it is important not to think in too linear and determinist a fashion that a crime against humanity constitutes anything more than the occasion for victim status. Between the crime and the victim there is the problem of its real, if not its reality, which the crime lets pass in silence, of which it makes a "blank," or which it understands sordidly as complicity or cowardice. The victim is one of the great theoretical inventions of the twentieth century, but one that, as is often the case, does not find its thought or its concept right off the bat. For our part, we formulate it as a "conjecture" destined to force the hesitating and unclear discourse of philosophy. The twentieth century contested the concept of man by struggling against it universally and by every means possible. Philosophy having accomplished a critique of humanism, the human sciences took over and hurried to destroy not only humanism but man himself. His essence and his existence were contested at both extremes by animality, divinity, and a third term, technics. They were put into play in a gigantomachy that even Plato could not have foreseen, between man's reduction to the vital space on the one hand and, on the other, the infinite transcendence of his relation with the one God. Anthropology, molecular biology, and paleontology dissolve man into sequences and reticular effects, into genetic and cultural bifurcations, multiplying and juxtaposing human families. Biotechnologies no longer know where to set the limit of the beginning or of the completion, or the death, of the human species in the animal kingdom and in relation to itself. This transparency of man – the loss of his opacity and his dissolution in chemistry, biology, and physics, in all the possible histories and cultures – reduces him to the state of vanishing traces. Contested as well by biotechnological cloning, man was brought to his final limits. The rational animal was dismembered – no longer anything but a system of effects and dimensions – systemism and complexity being among the final efforts to recapture the exhausted paradigm on the edge of the abyss. The idea finally emerges of the possibility of quantitatively or industrially destroying or producing him.

However, it is not for philosophy to content itself with a statement of a phenomenon's occasions and from that to induce generalities, but rather to seek if nothing else its real possibility or its principles in the depths of the human being rather than in extraneous causes. For this reason, we no longer have any other solution in the desert that man has become but to *put him forward as the object of a prior-to-the-first axiom for a theory of the victim and a deduction of the intellectual's acts of protection.* But this understanding of man as an axiomatic entity, free from cumbersome and indistinct predicates, certainly cannot stop at this formalism following which it would side with a final philosophical decision, hoping to escape into the clouds of an idealism or the effects of a materialism. It is doubtless necessary to recognize that it is as much an axiomatizable material as the real of a subject that holds this axiom under its proper condition, as if it were a formal materiality without at all being a philosophical auto-position or a topological torsion, which would only record and repeat the problem. Let us advance as a suggestion the term "oraxiom" to describe our non-humanist method of access to humans. Why?

On a theoretical plane, three current solutions make it difficult to approach the problem of man and victim without misunderstanding. Having become dominant conjuncturally, they should be indicated by their symptomatic character: (1) the creationist reaction as a symptom of a lost paradigm, without a doubt the most dangerous regression, but interesting for its permanent and hallucinatory confusion of the radical axiomatic identity, which makes up the essence of the human-in-person, with the unity of a creative transcendence; (2) the diehard imagination of science fiction that creates a putative human in yet a different way, confusing the vanishing-being of the subject with that of man, which it reduces to android and humanoid states. The hypothesis proposed here, of the duality of Man-in-person and the subject it clones non-biologically, recognizes in the human the necessity of an Indivisibility-without-unity, which it extracts from creationism, and of a being-vanished, more than absent, vanished-without-vanishing, which it extracts from science fiction. However, the solution is not in the synthesis of creationism or intelligent design, even the most well-informed, and science fiction: that would still be a philosophical artifact, but in a duality or a complementarity that we call "unilateral"; (3) finally, the politico-historical model of the victim, the defeated of the local revolt, the one crushed by repression, the excluded or the illegal immigrant of contemporary societies doomed to migratory flux, anguish, and the porosity of borders. This is certainly the most extensive and the most diversified historical material of the current century following the great persecutions of the previous, a persecution that itself has become multiple. Hence the emergence of philosophies of the "event," which took the place of thought concerning the victim and contributed to its forgetting or its abandonment to the human sciences. Two of them made history in the twentieth century and record – as always with philosophies, after the fact – in opposing ways, but not without affinity, the uneven and terrible course of the previous century. Heidegger, on the one hand, calls for and celebrates the advent of the principle of the German people as order and will on the spatio-historical stage. Badiou, on the other hand, at the end of the twentieth century, reinstates the Maoist order in conceptual philosophy by a resurrection of dialectical materialism, which is accompanied by a philosophy of the decision and an ethics of fidelity restricted to the trace of the event. These are both obviously thoughts of force – the one a totalitarian force in the vital space-time, the other the force of authoritarian exception in the modern space-time of knowledge. They admire only the founding heroes and legislators of cities or of worlds, and have nothing but scorn, denial, or at best indifference for democracy and victims. In these ways of thinking Being, nothing is demanded of the subject but to walk in already worn tracks. They cannot render justice to victims because their context is too narrow and reduced to the enclosure of the world, indeed of worlds, as if the multiplication of worlds truly changed the dimension of thought and opened onto anything other than a supplement of transcendence. Only a non-philosophy of humans as immanent victims, not as all-victim, can oppose the ontological anonymity of things, of bodies, and of historical events. Obviously, the disadvantage of appealing to victims is the possibility of creating a misunderstanding and leading philosophers "into the temptation" of dissension. But we have no other vocabulary at our disposal.

How can we still think "Man" in spite of everything, in spite of the collapse of humanism, followed by the vanishing of "Man" amid modern sciences [*savoirs*], science fiction, and theories of the event? And in what sense is Man, who no longer has objectivity and is dissolved in mixtures of knowledge and concepts, still thinkable? This dissolution is for us a symptom to be interpreted. We need a thought that retains Man, but as having lost all his attributes. Let us then write this hollow man with axioms: Man is no more than the first term, indeed prior-to-the-first and thus indefinable naturally or philosophically; he needs axioms that are undoubtedly special, ones that testify if not to his reality then to his real potency, "oraxioms." However, axiomatization is here that of the field, postulated as a new empirical experience [*empirie*], of anthropology and the human sciences. Moreover, the problem does not amount to an absolute void of philosophy. There is indeed a reality or a conceptual materiality of Man, but a generic or reduced one. Man's disappearance is not relative or absolute; it is, as we say, radical: *he is withdrawn into himself, into his radical immanence – this is his non-consistency or his In-person insistence.* It is necessary to accept the thought that Man is vanished [*évanoui*], radically lost (in his own identity) but not absolutely lacking "to" his representation, and to say this according to this being-disappeared [*être-disparu*]. He doesn't exist anymore in the sense that one could attribute to him visible and itemized properties, his representation having been destroyed, but he *insists* by his effects, like a black box that only signals by its inputs and outputs. It is neither an object nor even an anonymous for-itself, but a generic Identity separated unilaterally, a without-relation including a relation that participates complementarily in it without damaging it.

The defense of humans

It seems it is not only God who has abandoned us, or history and the ideologies it has carried along, it is also philosophy, insofar as it has always been a masked theo-dicy, its preparation or its consequence. Philosophy has become insufficient – it had to recognize or deny this – through an excess of "sufficiency" to ensure that which seems to us to be the first task of an ethics: *the defense of humans divided up or divided against themselves.* Formulating this axiom of the human immanence of ethics is enough to require defining their a priori defense against their own natural or spontaneous usage, their "in-world" usage of their means, for example that of the old legislative Reason, which was itself one of the ethical and anti-ethical means of human existence. Ethics requires an internal reorientation of means and their usage according to the safeguarding of life. Even the hierarchy of Good and Evil will have been only a means to oppress and threaten human life. Thus, it does not "suffice," when it is not contradictory, to want to recapture this disaster of an ambiguous thought or of a compromised subject incapable of a stable ethics by gods less cruel or less barbarous as spectators, by means of a will submitting itself to the transcendence of

Reason, or by a "modernized" dialectical materialism, when it is not a supplement of conscience or memory, as if any of them had any effect on the scourge of History, which ceaselessly beats them back. As inefficacious a procedure as calling to a God even more silent than "hidden." Philosophy teaches us that there is nothing but bodies, languages, and truths, and is happy to discover that they are multiple, except that there is the human exception, as ordinary as it is (and because it is ordinary), whose effects on the whole extent of creation will have to be re-evaluated.

We already knew from the cries of victims and from the courage of certain heretics – perhaps without quite knowing it because of a sanctifying philosophy – that in God was concealed the Grand Persecutor. The true atheism is not as simple as philosophy imagines it to be. It occurs in two stages: the banal refusal to believe in a God is self-contradictory and satisfies those who think little, but the refusal to believe in a good God is the true rebellion. There is always a God lying in ambush, preparing his return in whatever negation is made of his existence, even a materialist one, but it is important that it be a malicious God, a thesis that only an "ultra"-religious heresy can face. The atheism of indifference is weak and lays down its arms along with its speech to philosophy; the second is a strong heresy, the "non-" theological radicalization of a malicious God, his extension to every divinity that would appear as One or Multiple, as Sole and Great or even as natural and pagan.

We no longer want to be Survivors of the philosophical disaster. Why survivors of philosophy? Religions are the matter of the world, its dark depths, but philosophy

is its spokesperson and its form, the thought-world par
excellence. We cannot handle the two separately as if
religions were self-sufficient without the philosophical
apparatus, as if philosophy could be independent of
the attraction of religions. When it is understood that
philosophy is a rational mythology become indispensable and planetarily hegemonic, a thought that never
admits to being outdated [*dépassée*] because it is racing
ahead [*dépassante*], that it is made to resist all counter-
examples and refutations as if it were a reasoning and
perhaps rational hallucination, that it is the argued
system of its own self-defense like a belief impervious to
the doubt it brings about, that it is its own protestation
of good faith and of its love of truth, then it is no longer
necessary to bother with an internal auto-critique or an
external hetero-critique, such as undertaking to limit
its sufficiency to a precise point, arguing indefinitely
against it for the right to treat it with a certain local
exteriority, as do materialisms. Full of doubt, which is
nothing but a medium for its sufficiency, philosophy
of its own accord cannot expose itself to anything but
a transcendental quietism. This is not enough for it to
relinquish the weapons of reason to Man-in-person
instead of persisting in giving reasons for Man. We do
not "ask for" this philosophical quietism, rather we
hypothesize from it another, one that lies at the heart
of every human action and is commanded of us as if by
an ultimatum, like a relation of indifference pushed to
a relation-without-relation to every possible philosophy
or religion. And we ask whether the victim, forgotten
for having been overexposed, would not be this ultimatum, which calls philosophers, some of whom have
become intellectuals, to a certain immanent non-acting,

which puts them on the same level as victims rather than in the busy commerce of opinions.

The problematic of material formalism

We introduce the concept of "Victim-in-person." It is more a question of a universal symbol – as, for example, the "Name of the Father" – under which it is appropriate to place the defense work of the intellectual, himself understood as an imitation or clone of the victim. It is not the local victim ideologically generalized or absolutized. Man-in-person is the root of the victim, its condition of-the-last-instance. It is rather the link between the two, the link to persecution and to victimization sustainable by Man, who, as generic, is not the factual or historical victim. There is no longer any unitary cause or auto-production of victims, in contrast to what some philosophies might think based on History. That is an extreme and vicious hypothesis, which we must find the means to eliminate. One does not want to defend a victimary interpretation of history and add it onto philosophy, to contrast a "victimodicy" to theodicy, but rather to think the victim's minimum possible real, that is to say, to think *according to the victim*. A victimological reductionism of History, its criminal staging, would be a return to philosophical representation and to its media complacencies, even though we would prefer to see it from the point of view of the defeated rather than of the victors, of the weak rather than of the strong, even if the weak are the only ones strong enough to defend themselves, that is, to "rise up." Such is the principle of intellectual work when it is no longer vicious or circular: to act and speak for the victim-in-the-world according to the Victim-in-person, which is never an object about which one could make a decision. Far from being a unitary formula ("We are all victims," a self-contradictory formula), it is a unilateral duality, which governs the form-axiom of every intellectual action in defense of victims. But to understand it, it is necessary to invert it in favor of the primacy of the real, to not yield on the fact that it is Man-in-person that makes possible but not sufficient the victimization of subjects.

The Victim-in-person is a formal symbol for the most concrete human subject insofar as it *sustains* a relation to the world, which for us is the form of philosophy, alone in worlding. However, humans are not defined as such by this relation, reflection, or consciousness of the object, to which they relate only in an occasional and relatively contingent manner. Victim status conjugates two very different but complementary causalities: an ultimate non-acting real, which authorizes a second causality, that of the world, to be exercised against it, to extend without limits its relation of desire and of human conquest. The victim forces us to discover at the core of its generic passivity an inversion of classical phenomenological intentionality, such that it is now the world that transcends or transgresses towards man, and not man towards the world, to which he is instead indifferent or foreclosed. As a result, the victim has the force that limits this criminal hatred the world bears it; the victim protects man from hate by making this hate appear a hallucination or an appearance, although a terribly objective one, ridding it, and humans as well, of the obsession with the world. There is no contradiction between these two effects, but two logics. The one, occasional and relatively autonomous, the philosophico-theological as a form-world, is in the end included in the other, which is radically autonomous and properly generic.

Let us begin with the traditional philosophical combination, "the rational animal." This formula signifies not a simple duality but a triplicity, the physical nature of man as being or body, but also as physicist or creator of physical knowledge, and finally the unity of the two, which is the third term, man as *naturally* a philosopher. It is thus a game, like physics as a science, or like philosophy. Thus understood, such a triplicity is hierarchizing and dis-equalizing, or grows accustomed to the final profits of philosophical rationality, which redoubles and appropriates the physical determination. To obtain the generic rather than the philosophical concept of humans as condition of-the-last-instance of an ethics, we must assume that these terms function differently, according to other relations. We must assume: (1) that the physicist as a natural being or physical object and the physicist as a rational or philosophizing being no longer fall under traditional philosophical rationality in their relation, nor do they determine one another according to the same univocal model of causality as that of philosophy; (2) that these are nothing but variables or parameters that define a new space for ethics in which they are reciprocally determined in an unequal and above all, this time, irreversible way, their inverse products being no longer equal or commutable, nor attributable to one and the same object – man. And thus, that there is no longer a transcendent identity or a unique and anonymous essence of the quasi-physicists that humans are, but instead a multiplicity or an individual diversity in which all members are *equally of mankind in-the-last-instance*; (3) that their unity or fusion is no longer overdetermined by philosophy, which introduces hierarchies, but under-determined by a mode of rationality we will call, following others, "quantum-oriented" – we will define it. It is to cease binding humans to a dis-equalizing philosophical essence and to conceive of them as a generic function of these two variables in relation within a quantum matrix. This matrix binds humans neither exclusively to animal nature ("ethics with a biological foundation") nor to the rational nature of this animal. Exclusively, that is to say, equally to their mixture under the rational domination of Logos and thus of philosophy.

In this way, the victim is formalized generically in what will be a matrix, an instrument that no longer pertains to philosophy alone and to its modes of conceptual reasoning.

1. We understand by victims those neutralized or without-life lived experiences [*vécus*], the *Erlebnisse* rather than the categories of individuals, even if these lived experiences are localizable according to those individuals. The non-individual lived experiences of the being-exploited, of the being-excluded, those of the being-murdered, of the being-persecuted, of the being-humiliated, and not, as history and philosophy – united in their shared empiricism – do too quickly, exploited, excluded, murdered, persecuted individuals, who are the occasional bearers of those non-individual lived experiences and who belong complementarily to the second causality.
2. Additionally, and this is essential, there is an original objectivity of these lived experiences, typical of an

interfering or undulatory materiality. We define it by means, even algebraic ones, that subtract it from the corpuscular materialism of bodies, even those dialectically divided and subjectivated. *Here, the thought of victims is not, to make a point of comparison, a mathematizing materialism, but rather materialized algebra in the service of a generic matrix.* The materialist dialectic (Badiou) remains an idealist enterprise, an ideal genesis of subjects as bodies. If for it there are only bodies and language, except that there are truths, for the material formalism implemented here there are only lived experiences and algebra, except that there is also, instead of their opposition, the algebraic objectivity of human lived experiences. Objective knowledge as "idempotence" and "complex number" is compatible with lived experience; this duality of components and this fusion is necessary to convince us of the real suffering of victims and of their force of uprising, which can only be understood physically by calling on wave modeling. We formalize the victim through the fusion or superposition of means that generically conjugate science and philosophy, formalism, and lived experience in a "material formalism."

Overexposed victim and superposed victim

Giving it a generic but non-unitary concept does not divide but dualizes the victim in a complementary way between its two "sources," the "in-person" and the "in-the-world," the second form being occasional and in the end included in the first. There are victims, but how do we know that there are, and under what guise, supposing that they are not sufficient to appear of their own accord? Do we have concrete evidence of evil that is not a simple Idea? We move from the *overexposed* or over-represented victim to the victim that we name according to a method of thought taken from quantum physics, which serves us as a scientific model, *superposed*, or again, from the victim-image to the victim-in-person or lived victim, the one that the intellectual in his person must revive and clone rather than repeat.

First of all, we have only the testimony said victims bring with them, which assures us, far more concretely than the philosophical transcendentals of Good and Evil, of their material or lived reality. Victims are the vector of evil, its body-vector, evil in flesh and bone insofar as it was effectuated and written into the materiality of lived bodies, inscribed into human flesh by force. The materialist exaltation of bodies, even dialectically sub-jectivated ones, is too philosophical and thus too idealist an argument compared to the human victim. Even the celebration without restraint of philosophizability or "worldification" of all things is an act of supplementary victimization. For the honor of thought, it is as crucial to break the old pagan identification with philosophy or the world as it is to break the alliances with the God of the monotheisms, be it of Israel, of Christianity, or of Islam, to which recent intellectuals tend to limit them-selves, as do philosophers – in particular the first among them, Heidegger – who dare to carry out a Greek ethnic purification of thought.

By tilting the ethics of God or of Being towards its victims in order to henceforth redefine them as deprived of philosophical and theological salvation, we renounce not only classical onto-theology, but also its contempo-rary scraps of idealism and materialism, still attached to religious transcendence and alterity, which guarantee subjects their status as bodies at once divided and closed, as corpuscles. It is thus necessary to supplement on a theoretical plane the generic ethical axiom and to set down the being-superposed or interfering, the being-of-vector of Jewish, Greek, and Christian predicates that defines ethics or states its negative consequence. This complement summarizes our "generic imperative" in theory and in ethics, *neither a Greek nor a Jewish predicate, which are only means to interfere vectorially*. This watchword is part of an a priori defense of humans against a misuse of their works, and makes visible the difficulty hidden in that formula of immanence, "humans themselves," handling humans with Greek or Judaic means or predicates, but as generic subjects without Greek or Judaic finality other than that of putting the world and its bodies under condition. The only generic "finality," if it is one, is that of humans as the under-determining Last Instance, that is, quantumly superposing the theoretical means that are used to describe them. Predicates do not exhaust the subject, which is foreclosed to them, provided that we conceive of the subject as an under-determining Last Instance. This is not to forget concrete and fleshly victims in a new generality, but to refuse by this formalism to mimetically or specularly duplicate them in theory, a duplication its generic meaning rejects. The cloning of victims in the form of intellectuals will be something completely different from a mimetic rivalry.

But how do we know that there are or that these are victims? Do we have a necessary if not sufficient reason to recognize them in their actuality and more profoundly in their "possibility" or "virtuality"? Evil is *simultaneously concrete and formal* beyond the media empiricity of victims. The victim has always been an *object, but not of knowledge*. It only begins to be one at best as an object of pity or lamentation, of memory and rituality, and more and more of mutual assistance, being thus marked out for a literature of intellectuals by Logos, which for its part flees towards the religious horizon. There have been and there will be victims, so speaks philosophy; it is a regrettable history, which "gives us something to think about," the causes of which it is only just possible to show, and which, moreover, put the courage and heroism of individuals to the test. There is without a doubt, as certain philosophers of knowledge would say, an a priori *universal* of the victim, *for* it. But these reasons are a priori just like they are in the philosophical style, where the a priori exists in an originary continuity, incorrectly interrupted, for example a transcendental one, with phenomena to be elucidated or explicated. Hence, this ideological cloud, these blurred notions, improperly spread out on the basis of a compassion understood as pity, with some nuances through which one's name is cleared, which are the best means to drown the victim in the rest of creation and perhaps to persecute it a second time, all the while absolutizing and perhaps absolving our culpability.

There are victims, this much is obvious, but this way of acknowledging them and giving standing to them in thought means that, thus represented, they are only presupposed, subject to doubt and forgetting, to denial, philosophical revisionism [*négationnisme*], whatever philosophy might say of them and whatever their media overexposure and their becoming absolute make us believe. We only know them as victims because *there is*, if you will, firstly Man-in-person as the real kernel of the simply radical (in-person) and not absolute (in-the-world) victim. The instance that ensures that the victim must be radically and not absolutely a priori, through superposition and not through dialectics, this reason must be able to precede the victim in-prior-priority, even by being "separated-without-separation" or foreclosed to it, and in this sense render the victim really possible without depending on some sort of continuity with the victim. Still, *there is no* Man as a straightforward and hazy presupposed horizon or fact, an object immediately forgotten and idealized in substitutes such as memory. You will not make of the victim an absolute or a mode of the absolute (against Judaism); you will not make of it an accident of history or the world (against philosophy). When it is a question of Man, the a priori is no longer that of knowledge but of "reality" or, better still, of "real-without-reality," of "non-sufficient necessity." Unlike God, generic Man is universally necessary but not sufficient according to an "ontological argument"; it is the Real as a priori *for* the world. Put another way, the generic human a priori is not simply "formal" even though it has an element of "form" (form of the reception of the world assumed nonetheless to be in itself and for itself, of the givenness of the world reduced to an objectivity of appearance by Man-in-person). Even if the mechanisms of victimization are more complex and make the efficacy of the world intervene through its philosophical form, it is Man insofar as he does not exist in the world or insofar as he is not philosophizable that is the world's ultimate condition. And he insists virtually rather than not existing or appearing *ex nihilo* symmetrically to divine "creation." The new materialist dialectic (Badiou) uses an argument that looks a lot like the "ontological" argument, and which is the sort of proto-transcendental or "inexistent" void that enables it to do without all finite humanity (which is constituent) and, in the end, deny the status of the victim.

Man-in-person is the last but non-sufficient cause, the of-the-last-instance cause that under-determines and manifests the worldly victim as human and tears it out of the world. As for memory, it is the element of a ghostly and spectral existence of the persecuted, but Man as generic subject is the non-memorial a priori that gives victims their real feature [*trait de réel*] and not only an existence liable to doubt. Neither the duty of work nor the duty of memory are adequate to the Victim-in-person, which is instead that which under-determines victims in-the-last-instance.

Justice according to victims: from the tribunal-form to the matrix-form

What do we gain by formulating as a rule the non-separability of the victim and its monotheistic concepts, victimological excesses included, in order to better separate them afterwards according to a whole other method, a priori reattaching the victim to Man as to the real rather than to its representations, which it under-determines, separating it this time from the victimo-logical mixes? Without a doubt, we gain a more rigorous understanding of the victim as an object of continuous double victimization by onto-theo-logy taken in an extended sense. Then, there is the possibility of a struggle against philosophical victimology and not only against victimary ideology, which is too narrow a motivation to assure us of its mutation rather than its summary rejection.

If humans, as their victim status shows, are complementarily in-person and in-the-world, this hypothesis implies transferring ethics from the undoubtedly depleted philosophico-theological ground of providence and its materialist substitutes onto the ground of the universal victims of philosophy, ideologies, and religions. The victim of a God who is presented as good, explicitly or implicitly under the mask of materialism, and precisely because He is presented as good, surely cannot give rise to a simple paradox, solvable in philosophy. We must relocate the basis of thought from the so-called good God to the victims of his real maliciousness. A true "theoretical conversion" of philosophical belief in favor of a new lived experience, in all likelihood that of faith freeing itself from this belief, is obviously necessary in order to admit that philosophy, which is a structured and solid thing, which allows it to be distinguished even in its gossipy usages and which in any case gives us the only linguistic means we have, can be incriminated in its turn. For it is no longer a question of simply critiquing or deconstructing philosophy, of leading it to its death or to its end, and even less of exalting it, but rather of bringing it not before the victim summoned directly to vengeance – that would be an ethical catastrophe and the ruin of justice – but before generic Man whom we make the *real and thus a priori condition*, so that there are victims, and more broadly, a thought that does justice to them without falling into the All-victim or the victimology of the human sciences.

Is the tribunal of Reason now before the tribunal of the Victim? The Victim-in-person is no longer, if it ever was, a tribunal for philosophy, for its betrayal and abdication, any more than Evil is for Good. As an instrument of justice, we substitute for the tribunal-form, juridical and institutional and founded on a displacement of individual vengeance, the matrix-form, which is theoretical and practical in theory. The victim itself is ordered in relation to Man-in-person as determining in-the-last-instance every relation of justice and, more particularly, every "intellectual" evaluation. Perhaps one could make the hypothesis, which it is no doubt necessary to pursue, that justice according to the Victim-in-person, which is generic rather than philosophical, results on the one hand from the conjugation of these variables, which are institutional justice (derived from displaced individual vengeance) and the care of intellectuals (who take up the victims as a philosophical concern), and on the other hand from an imaginary or complex coefficient of quantum usage, which indexes the inverse products of these variables. In the generic state, these inverse products of the properties of justice are obviously non-commutative, and bear witness to the under-determination exercised by victims on intellectuals and philosophers alike, under-determined intellectuals in contrast to the over-determined intellectuals of philosophy. It is understood that if the generic justice of the oppressed, humiliated, and defeated contains a moment of cloning of the intellectual and philosophical subject, it cannot be a question of either a mimetic rivalry between the intellectual and "his" victim or a body-subject dialectically divided but still specularly functioning in doublet of itself.

What do victims expect from us? What form of "recognition" if not an understanding rather than a memory, and obviously rather than revenge? Perhaps they expect

an unhoped-for gift from us who, after having persecuted them, believe that we have done a lot by giving
them a bit of memory or duty, a low form of conscience,
of bad conscience? Traditionally, memory contemplates
the victim, either by the imperative to memory, or by
the work of memory; this is the equivalent of the the-
oricism that upholds the matching types of philosophy,
idealism and materialism. Instead of being projected
into the sky of Ideas, they are projected into the earth.
The eidetic site and the site of the dead are symmetrical.
They exchange their power, which is that of duplicity:
a double sky solidified from the concept or from luminous objectivity, a double monument of the tomb and
of black materiality. And what if they expected thought
instead of this memory reserved for the waste of history,
for all that we pass off as losses and gains? And a true
work of transformation, and why not of "resurrection"
– we shall come to this – rather than a hermeneutic of
specters and phantoms? Even for victims, a rigorous
method is required to which even the rituals of memory
attest in their own way. That memory is not of the order
of victims in the strict sense, but rather of the order
of the mixes they form with their representations; it is
the victimo-logical complex with its Judaic, Christian,
and Islamic modalities, its persecuted or its martyrs.
This material is a symptom for a treatment that is at
once theoretical and practical, and that appears on the
surface like a vast de-Judaization, de-Christianization,
de-Islamicization of notions that touch on man, as a
new form of what was once called a de-mythization.
That, however, is only one facet of the procedure to be
implemented, the most negative and thus still the most
dependent on philosophy. Since philosophy consists

of interpreting it after the fact within the perspective opened by Man as given a priori without-givenness, the victim will receive a generic body more fully by superposition, for example, a non-Judaic one that has one side of de-Judaization, and so on. Kant's formula regarding men and their dignity, treating them "as an end and not only as a means," has not yet yielded all of its effects. On the one hand, Kant supposes that the problem is resolved because he speaks of the "other" (how does he know that the victim is an "other" to me, something that involves many presuppositions?). On the other hand, as a rationalist he separates the end and the means as two instances without perceiving the constitutive ambiguity of the means in his formulation "not only," which affects the very identity of means as a double relation to the end, but which does not affect the end itself. Neither his anthropology nor his theory of the subject, at best transcendental, is able to account for the real superpositional identity of a subject, whose division only appears in its relation of use to the means.

The generic ultimatum

Our imperative, the Victim-in-person as taken from victimology under the human condition of-the-last-instance, eludes the simple categorical and rational imperative of humanity and its definition through the coupling of "end/means." This oraxiom is imperative in its character as ultimatum, and categorical not through what it prescribes in the positive but through what it "rejects," through that to which Man is foreclosed, or which or resists every form of totality, in particular the set of monotheisms to which philosophy testifies and which it formalizes. Its real condition breaks this imperative in two through a unilateral complementarity, refusing to analytically and/or synthetically link imperativity and categoricity, necessity and sufficient totality, refusing to deduce the second from the first, as long as it is not simultaneously "sufficient," and even more the first from the second. The victim, at the core of the philosopher who denies it, rejects religions only to make use of them no longer as belief or totality but as consummation. To link the victim and the scenarios that philosophy proposes for it without a vicious circle, all that is absent between them is the real, Man-in-person as Last Instance, which can explain a certain necessity and ability, itself under worldly occasion, for humans to experience themselves as victims without being exhausted by an absolute necessity. The generic real is precisely not absent as a synthesis that should have but has not been effected. This synthesis is in any case already given with Reason, which is at the heart of the categorical imperative, which the victim uses in a spontaneously philosophical way. Nor is the generic real absent the way an empirical man or an intelligible freedom is absent, but rather through its "real absence," which is not an absence of perception or representation, interior to these and measured by them, but through the refusal of its generic nature to allow itself to be seized and identified by them. Man-in-person is no longer identical to the victim, nor does it contain the victim analytically, as if Man-in-person has always and necessarily been the victim according to a transcendent logic without being able to do anything considerable against its state. It is a non-positional refusal (of the) self, an immanent or lived "non-" that knows itself [*se sait*] but without apprehending itself [*se connaître*] or possessing itself [*s'avoir*] as what it is. Humans contrast this "non-" to the intervention of philosophy in the very act by which they accede to that claim, or mobilize it the better to contain it. Put differently, generic Man is the Last Instance, which manifests – without creating it – the philosophical act drawn up against the Victim at the moment when the latter orders that act to serve as a simple means. In this way, we explain how it could at the same time render possible the victim status offered to adversity and the victim's ultimate possibility of resisting this state *in spite of everything*.

It is obviously not for one and the same reason that the victim is offered, from further away than its actuality, to crime, and that it can resist it – that would be a vicious circle. That which affects the victim who has "already" resisted is ambiguous or could be read in two different ways, ones that are not dialectically opposed, just unilaterally complementary. The victimizing gesture can be lived by the victim as absolute or in itself, crushing and invincible, or else generically as an objective appearance, which the victim has already resisted by the very fact of manifesting it. There are no reciprocal relations, only a unilateral non-relation between Man-in-person that is the lived experience (of the) victim and the individual victim identifiable by such and such an "accident." A one-way complementarity distributes the phenomenological work of manifestation, the non-positional manifested (of the) self, the self-possessing (of the) self that the victim has without the knowing it(self), and which the victim will likewise learn to know and to de-potentialize by leaning on its misfortune as a symptom coming from further away than itself, or in prior-priority. Measured according to philosophical dualities, the Victim-in-person (a way of assembling this unilateral duality of functions) is in-prior-priority in relation to the all-victim or to the not-all victim, which are the two principal poles between which theoretical victimology oscillates. The Victim-in-person is thus the generic human insofar as it is capable of being, without a vicious circle, at once radical victim and resistant to the oppressor, capable of *rising up* and of bringing about the transformation of an object or an event of the world. "At once," the victim is of it-"self," which is to say in-the-last-instance against the vicious circle with which the duality of its object threatens it.

Glorious bodies

Our matrix, for example, is neither a "class" nor a "set" nor a "world," as dialectical materialisms have proposed, but that which conjugates and weakens these knowledges to reduce them to the state of simple means for the defense of victims, which was not at all the case in their spontaneous and philosophical usage. The matrix indexes the uprising and the struggle that follows upon a complex or "imaginary" number necessary for super-position or vectoriality, and complementarily, upon variables or the effectuations of variables. The imaginary number and its "vectorial" (rather than positively *vectorielle*) representation substitute their insurrectional objectivity for the subjectivity of the transcendental imagination (Kant and Fichte), but, more profoundly still, for the macroscopic objectivity of the logics that are the transcendental of classes or even of worlds (Badiou). In this materialism, even the most objective bodies remain in the transcendental dimension, which is to say in the dimension of (double) philosophical transcendence or of the doublets with which it functions. For us, this is the crucial problem. From the theoretical decision taken on this problem – either the transcendental, even logicized and topologized, or the real immanence of Man/Victim-in-person – the victim will be murdered a second time by philosophy and the self-assured good conscience of dialectical materialism, or respected as a victim "once each time." A transcendental materialist returns to a sort of a priori or to a conclusion without the proto-premise of the Last Instance and its radical immanence. Respect for the victim consists of treating it as a human offered to the world as possibly or occasionally murderable, persecutable, humiliatable, and thus also capable of rising up against the adversary and thereby of indicating or naming it. Indicating or naming the one who kills you or exploits you is the uprising itself, the radical or prior-to-the-first beginning of resistance. Man, and thus the Victim-in-person, cannot be confused with the beings of the world or with the bodies indexed to worlds or subjects "interpellated" by such a class, which are distributions interior to the philosophico-religious form.

We are obliged to modify the materialist concept of the body and even that of the divided body-subject (without mentioning that of "worlds"), which remains in the spirit of a properly corpuscular or macroscopic description, whereas the generic matrix is quantum in spirit and implies the essential transformation of the corpuscle into a particle and the world into a system of vectors. It is not exactly a question of a microscopic rather than a macroscopic dimension: quantum theory, formalized generically, can be invested in apparently macroscopic phenomena. It is a problem of lived vectorial structures rather than of objects in themselves. The defeated of history and more generically the rebels in the world, therefore beyond historical situations of reaction and political conservation, cannot be named and vectorialized except by the occasional reference to a context of philosophico-religious doublets. For us, the most significant uprisings are those that, like undulatory phenomena of propagation, pertain to humans as such or "in-people" rather than to their specification as proletariat; they are at least as much the uprisings of the Gnostics and heretics, of the Anabaptists and the messianic movements, as those that respond to a causality localizable according to the classically political criteria used in the human and social sciences, and even in Marxism in the form of historical materialism. Neither localization nor globalization in a "world," in an "ethnic group" or a "community," or even in a "social class" can define these movements, which imply a different logic than the one divided "into" philosophical transcendence and its macroscopic doublets, because they call into question the hegemony of philosophy and its Platonizing practice as a spectral image of mathematics. These divisions occupy intellectual philosophers who get lost in this labyrinth, but for our problematic they are too narrow and limited. They pertain precisely to a transcendent(al) logic of worlds or of classes, not yet to the most extensive and most overdetermining religious dimension, which is not taken into account as such. That said, from an empirical and historical point of view, the glory of the defeated is obviously relative, but it is also its clandestine nature that operates and can serve to measure their effect. It is for this reason that we will avoid making the intensity of existence the criterion for an event and its impact, which is not measured by its actuality or actual existence any more than by the memory that it transforms, which plays like the shuttle-cock of history.

For these reasons of the religious context dominant in history and in the world, and for the theoretical reasons already mentioned, we define the body of the victim as a field of vectors according to, on the one hand, religious variables – sacrificial and resurrectional (we will come to this) – and, on the other hand, their indexation to an imaginary number as a glorious body. The glorious body is this ultimate or of-the-last-instance aprioric materiality, which serves as the form of reception and transformation for the philosophico-religious material. The Judaic concept of Man as persecuted, hostage or survivor, or the materialist but nevertheless ideal concept of body-subject, can be transmuted into that of modes of the glorious body, such that discourse can be made adequate to it within a generic operation of non-Christianization or non-Judaization of the victim. As for those Judaic, Christian, and Islamic notions in their monotheistic variety: after serving as symptoms and material, after having been inwardly inverted in favor of the prior-priority of Man, they complete the cycle of their mutation by being understood as historical models of interpretation of this axiomatization of thought according to the victim.

Repetition of bodies and resurrection of lived experiences

In the end, we distinguish two types of victims, two becomings capable of affecting them whatever the cause of their death: the repeated or survivor victim, and the arisen victim as a glorious body. On the one hand, the victim as interpreted by the world, condemned to survival even when supposed dead. Memorial survival is the maximum that philosophy and religion can offer, sometimes under the materialist mask of logic and mathematics; it is in reality a continued death or a victimization in-the-world. On the other hand, there is the victim interpreted according to its generic essence, if not repeated, at least arisen or "awakened," which is to say saved from continued victimization. The opposition here is no longer only between the immanence of philosophical science and existential repetition, as in Kierkegaard, but between all forms of repetition of and in transcendence and resurrection, which is more a revival of the generic lived experience as glorious lived experience rather than repetition as a reproduction of bodies.

The stumbling block is obviously the introduction of "resurrection," and worse still, of the arisen or "glorious" lived experience in a "non"-Christian or, in a certain sense, atheist thought. It is not an accident if contemporary philosophers, claiming their atheism more or less explicitly, try to formulate a Christianity without God, or an "atheist" Christianity. The risk is reducing Christianity to a kind of "cultural revolution," an event whose consequences are scrutinized without examining its real conditions, which are material rather than materialist, and algebraic rather than logical. These conditions have rendered more than possible the symbolic name of "Christ," living and more than living, lived *for and in* every man. This is not a Christological and somewhat Judaic deconstruction of Christian theology. We will need a complex or "imaginary" – in the non-miraculous, proto-quantum sense – interpretation of the Resurrection, one that is physical rather than idealist, and generic rather than philosophical. The resurrection has always been understood – we do not say misunderstood because where would the invention be? – according to the paradoxical common sense of a miracle oscillating between being and nothing, whether this miracle is explicitly theological or purely decisional. Either way, it is inseparable from the void or akin to the inapparent. We cannot forget the objection Jacobi made to Fichte, or the conjunction of idealism and materialism with nihilism. By its intrinsically in-person real, the victim is the counter-witness to nihilism, the same way that before it was the counter-example to creation *ex nihilo*. The victim carries with it resurrection, or rather the prior-to-the-first insurrection, against the dialectic of being and nothingness, which has no real or lived sense. The victim is a power of "awakening" or "reprise" in the order of the lived experiences opposed to the simple dialectical or differential repetition of survival. Survival reinforces transcendence, an act that exceeds death or persecution and prolongs the world, whereas insurrection, which is the root of resurrection, weakens or debases this transcendence of a world to the state of lived experience. The awakening invoked by the Gnostics corresponds to this experience of an insurrection that comes from further away than the life of victims crushed by the weight of the world. Victims don't survive by passing from life to lived-experience-without-life. The death of the old, individual body, standardized and established by philosophy and religion together, guaranteed by its insertion in the world, is at once (but in a unilateral and complementary way) the occasion of the insurrectional awakening and the effect of the insurrection that transforms bodies. For us-the-Gnostics and us-the-generics, this is the role of the intellectual: to help victims in this uprising, to imitate and prolong this uprising in the human dimensions of thought.

From pity to the principle of compassion

As for the affect that accompanies the victim, we will distinguish between pity and compassion. Pity for compassion because it is the affect at the source of care! Their confusion attests to a lack of theoretical sensibility. To take up a well-known thread, they are distinguished somewhat similarly to the way that fear before an object and anxiety before nothingness are distinguished (Kierkegaard and Heidegger), and are based on ontologically "opposed" principles. They implicate the lived experiences that relate to human subjectivities rather than to the anonymous entities of being, nothingness, and Being. They are fundamental for ethics rather than for ontology, without, however, tipping into the conception of Man as hostage of the Other (Levinas). Pity and compassion do not appeal to the theoretical objectivity of ontology, and even less to the hyper-objectivity in the manner of the I as hostage of God. These are the affects of immanence that have an effect and an echo in transcendence. They are not the affects first and foremost of transcendence, or theoretical affects that would have an echo in immanence. Fear and anxiety are different obstacles to speech and knowledge in a world, whereas pity and compassion are different obstacles to philosophical speech itself, and in any case to theory, but are also that which can transform them.

Within this great division, which must be refined further, properly ethical sensibility distinguishes among its objects those that are nevertheless inseparable from transcendence or that appear as combined once again with representation. These objects appear at the limit of a certain ecstatic distance, and appeal to a supposed universal shared by all creatures, as is life or the will-to-live. As internal as it is, pity is nevertheless directed at an object, however subjective. Compassion is much more intimate and secret, already separated. In compassion, unilateralizing separation from transcendence prevails over its relation to transcendence. As much as pity is a theologically dominated sentiment derived from piety and its interiority, which is linked to an exteriority, so compassion appeals to lived passivity, being felt, with a minimum of representation, from one individual to the next. Pity has a quantitative side, whereas compassion is given once each time as an operation that does not increase. It is an affect that runs from one subject to another by propagation rather than contagion. It is lived in another by me and as much as in me. It is a secret affect, which is not locatable and whose extensive trajectory cannot be traced, as it can be for pity. It possesses a fluidity that pity does not have, which fixes itself more quickly upon an object. Pity justifies itself on the one hand by its object and, on the other, by divine all-goodness or the shared universality of life, both of which command it. Compassion for humans, living or not, and hence for the rest of creation – the rest of an impossible All – does not have to justify itself by some sufficient reason, a final trace of which remains even in the compassionate discourse used by the media. But it is easier to squander volatile compassion with chatter than it is to squander pity, which abstains from it.

Endowed with a certain neutrality, even a form of objectivity reduced to the algebra of a vector, compassion is a function of a single lived wave, which includes – without ever rendering them a totality – the victim and the intellectual, who experiences compassion experimentally and not contemplatively. Why "experimentally," a term that seems quite inappropriate? Compassion is the fusion, in a non-representative space, of the victim and the thought attached to it; but we cannot forget, at the risk of an insipid Christian-humanist "sympathy," that this fusion is a superposition of the quantum order and that it comes through a collision of the essentially generic victim and the essentially philosophical intellectual, such that they are constrained to meet each other in this secret, clandestine collider, the Victim-in-person. Compassion cannot be a simply universal or rational principle. It is not a principle except in-the-last-instance, generic, that is, universal-without-reason and necessary-without-sufficiency. It is the formal materiality that under-determines as an ultimatum the actions of the intellectual and constrains them to submit to human immanence rather than to aspire to save it memorially by an excess of survival in the world. To sympathize "in" the victim is to interfere with its passivity, and this without establishing an intersubjective synthesis starting from the already given or still to be constructed body. From a logical point of view, compassion does not establish a pure analytical relation with the victim of which the intellectual is not an included mode, nor a synthetic relation within a superior body in which the intellectual would be "in command," or which the intellectual would steer. Put differently, worldly events are not determinant or sufficient to motivate anything but pity, and are nothing but simple occasions in the eyes of compassion. The encounter with a victim – a negated individual, humiliated, tortured, even excluded from humanity itself – as well as the encounter with a death attributed to the blind stupidity of nature or God, always a bit of a jealous spectator, is a phenomenon more like a collision than an accident in a technological circuit or a breakdown that resolves itself, and even more like a collision than an encounter with a kindly face or a smile. Such a collision of affects does not occur in the milieu of transcendence nor does it have the nature of a philosophical event. It remains within a milieu of interference and superposition.

The transcendent event, the one that occurs in the form of a flash, of an appearance/disappearance, and whose set-theoretical ontology proclaims that it belongs to itself, ends in an aporia given the identity of the decision and the undecidable, of the undecidable as that to be decided. But the immanent event of the collision in space is vectorial and it too calls for an undecidable decision, this time constituted and no longer determining. This philosophical aporia is part of the consequences, rather than being at the origin of the consequences. The majority of ethics are more like a decision to be taken according to a logical criterion, be it the logical form of the law commanding respect (as in Kant), or another logical form more complex than the classical one, or according to an All to be equaled. Being affected by a victim produces the effect of an imperative reduced to the form of an ultimatum not determined by what follows it or its consequences, the consideration or the precise taking into account of which would end up rendering it sufficient. It is not a law that would affect itself through the medium of sensibility. Its materiality cancels out rigorism (Kant) without falling into a substantial materiality of values (Scheler). Its algebraic formalism cancels out the old logical formalism of non-contradiction of the subjective maxim with the universal law, without resorting to a Christian foundation.

Radical passivity is the root of good practice. We distinguish reaction as repetition and *reprise, which confirms passivity without making it a reaction,* or which makes compassion out of passion. Because the generic subject is humankind in-person or a human multiplicity in-person, passion is straightaway compassion. Even victims have compassion for their executioner; compassion extends even to them. It alone can save them or bring them back into the realm of humans. Compassion is not the philosophical pity of animals participating in universal life. It is the final lived experience, the experience of the defeated that borders death and still gives it its meaning in-the-last-instance.

It is a modality of that which Marx, in a context and with intentions apparently distant but hardly more political, called a revolutionary (that is, insurrectional first of all) fusion of the masses and theory. Thus the problem of an under-determined thought is resolved by the real victim and not by philosophical victimology.

2

Media Intellectual and Generic Intellectual

First terms for a theory of intellectuals

We must create a stable vocabulary. In general, we will call "intellectual" the type exemplified in current affairs under that term, not individuals, but the a priori function that they fulfill. In this sense, "intellectuals" are the symptom of that which philosophy becomes when it takes victims to heart and takes care to attend to them and raise them to the status of principal object, between image and phantasm. We will again raise the problems of ethics from this conjuncture, from this node that links the victim and an intellectual agent under the ultimate authority of philosophy.

We will call a media intellectual, engaged or embedded,[1] he who uses media in order *to be invested in the media.* He uses media to expose the image of the

---

[1] In the original text, the word "embedded" appears italicized in parentheses, translating the French *embarqué* that precedes it. Henceforth we render *embarqué* as "embedded." [*Trans.*]

victim, from the oldest (the book, printed matter) to the most innovative or most revolutionary media, and under authority of the medium par excellence, which is philosophy – Voltaire and Zola, for example, and not just the current fringe of tele-intellectuals who represent the low watermark of this group. These intellectuals make philosophy the overdetermining medium of all ethics and justice, the only "world" or "transcendental" they offer to victims.

In contrast to these intellectuals, embarked on so fragile a skiff, subject to its shifts in angle, its pitching and tossing, buffets of wind from the storm [*coups de vent de l'événement*], we will distinguish "generic" (or "under condition," or even "non-standard") "intellectuals," who use philosophy out of necessity, but as a simple under-determined means, without finality as to the real of victims, ultimately dedicated to the prior-to-the-first defense of victims. They are under condition of humans and their capacity-to-be victims rather than being in the service of the "values" and "ends" of philosophy. Parallel to the necessary redefinition of the victim as human in-the-last-instance, this new hypothesis will define one of the successors of the philosopher, the non-philosopher, insofar as he defines himself ethically in relation to the victim and allows himself to be under-determined by the victim. If the "engaged intellectual" was not long ago the noble inheritor of Voltaire and Zola, we must remember that this lineage, subject to the shock of the crimes of the twentieth century, among which must be counted the historic suicide of Marxism, was split into two extremely divergent branches, one rallying to theoretical and mediatic liberalism, the other trying to revive what was revolutionary in communism. Even sketched schematically, this split, from our point of view, is a typical occurrence proper to the "philosophical decision," founded in these two extreme cases on the denial [*dénégation*] of the Victim-in-person. Since the "renegation" [*renégation*] and the renegades in use in Maoism are actually arisen from the dead, let us say, to change the word's meaning a bit, that all philosophers are renegades of victims or of humans.

The system of intellectual Reason

Intellectual Reason is a material but a priori instance, a system of gestures and operations that fulfills an intellectual function in an extended sense. Deployed in its four branches, it is an intervention (1) in the name of supposedly violated abstract values – justice, freedom, and human rights – whose substantiality remains indeterminate, (2) which appears as a defense in the aid of an isolated or collective individual, (3) in the form of speech and writing, (4) whose occasion is furnished by history or politics as current events or memory in a way at once contingent and persistent. At this stage, it is still a generality to be specified according to the two types already distinguished.

The deployed concept of intellectual Reason takes into account the whole structure that makes it work, and upon which the victim will soon be crucified a second time, that is, sacrificed by the embedded intellectual. The name "intellectual" thus refers less to an individual than a system of instances. The engaged intellectual must render these heterogeneous instances coherent; in particular, he must restore harmony to the two poles which occupy him, power and the victim, by subjecting the whole thing to a Principle of intellectual Reason, an Idea or an Ideal to which he aspires and which guides and legitimates his action. This ideal rather than the in-prior-priority real system gives rise to idealism as well as to materialism.

First of all, it is necessary to identify the form of polemical rationality of defense through discourse and writing (call, testimony, petition signing, etc.) that the intellectual exercises. Intellectual Reason is not political, aesthetic, scientific, or philosophical Reason. Above all, ethico-political or mixed, intellectual Reason is spontaneously hardly pragmatic, even though the intellectual is dedicated to a certain opportunism. As ethico-political rather than purely political, it appears as an a priori defense of individuals, groups, and communities, but it justifies itself above all by that which it defends and transfers onto the person of the intellectual. Like a lawyer specializing in human affairs at the convergence of politics, history, and ethics, the intellectual practices a sort of ecology of singular human life to be preserved – be it the life of a people in the case of genocide or of large supra-individual entities. This ecology is therefore decisive for establishing a generic ethics, even though it itself has a philosophical rather than generic essence. Its a priori is necessary and universal in a sufficient manner, and pertains to a particular or singular but not generic individual. Any scientist, artist, philosopher, local, or international collectivity – even the State itself – can fleetingly exercise an intellectual function.

If it is essential for the media intellectual to privilege the act of defense as primary in relation to the victim, which is a secondary and contingent occasion, the victim should have been prior-to-the-first and the very condition capable of determining the operations of defense. *But the embedded intellectual in fact orbits around power (which he must seduce to be able to limit), rather than around victims, whose defense becomes a pretext for the exercise of the intellectual's narcissism.*

The intellectual's traditional figure is associated with other agents, the pair of victim and oppressor, forming a classically philosophical triad of inseparables, the victimological triad; a quaternary if we add the production of writing and speech. As philosophical logic desires, all these heterogeneous and complementary instances must function together in a frictional and problematic synergy. Victim, persecutor, and intellectual are above all doomed to appearances, which are each time specific. The intellectual, too, is biased; the worthiness of the positions he takes does not protect him – on the contrary – from the appearance wherein the spontaneity of his practice encloses him. The intellectual is a mixed or multiple being that has no purity – purity to which he lays claim and which he puts on display – except through the ideal cause or the values he defends, and from which he derives appreciable benefit, in particular that of attaining the rather miserable reputation and dignity of a "philosopher." He achieves it in realizing in his person the function of schematism or of mediation, which his miscellaneous instances require.

The unease of intellectuals: their unhappy consciousness

This situation of the traditional intellectual is uncomfortable for two reasons, which pertain to the same unfortunate phenomenon of division or unease, of which the intellectual thinks himself to be the solution when he is in fact its enactment. Instead of generically merging or superposing himself with the victim for an experience that will not be a new contemplation but a unique knowledge that inextricably holds for both the victim and himself, he tries to identify with the victim, confusing superposition and identification, and in fact divides the world in two.

1. The intellectual's object is divided, between the historical individual that is the victim and abstract justice or the rights of man, between an apparently concrete and individual object and an object or end that is supposedly real but actually abstract and stemming from philosophy. It is an insoluble discord, sometimes a contradiction between the abstraction of justice or the rights of man that the intellectual defends and the occurrences or events, often questionable and unstable, which force him to intervene and which testify to the occasional contingency of his material. With this pair of indeterminate values and concrete victims, which seem to him to be determined and which are nothing but overrepresented, he thinks that he has an object and a role, which he tries to look after, to manage out of necessity statements of ethical intention and opportunistic philosophical mediations. But he does not yet have his specific or proper object; this object is the fusion-superposition of the victim and its theory in the Victim-in-person, with which he is not required to identify but which demands that he assume it as his immanent condition, the site and body of practice in which he dangerously tests out his own subjectivity. He has only an overly general

---

and inadequate object: the system of philosophy itself rather than the victim and the justice suitable to it, which here are nothing but a part of its discourse. This system cannot function except by an overrepresentation of the victim and a media overexposure of the intellectual himself through a reproduction of doublets he makes proliferate.

2. The pathos of division or of difference takes another form: the division of labor between victim and intellectual. The one is devoted to suffering or the primitive affects of imaginary re-action, like vengeance, and the other to means of expression, but with a bad conscience, the one to silence and the other to speech, however unhappy. The victim, powerless several times over, receives as his share overwhelming and paralyzing pain, and the intellectual receives power and the right to protest, without the initial pain, just bad conscience, another form of reaction. A sharing out of tasks, a veritable "division of labor," this distribution contains a moment of double reflection in the victim and in the intellectual, which generates the real content of victimary ideology. It is the worst imaginable, and yet it is justified, legitimated by philosophy which can do nothing but promote it. The victim is the "phenomenological" consciousness, which suffers and "works," and the intellectual is its witness and conductor, its guardian and defender, all tasks that are traditionally those of thought and which turn easily into ideology. "We, philosophers . . .," Hegel's cynical formula, has been replaced by "We, intellectuals," commensurate with these small-scale philosophers. Either they shamelessly turn a blind eye (but this is no longer as much

the case), or they display their compassion. This is the infernal couple of quasi-divine malediction that overwhelms the victim and the good–bad conscience of its defender. The intellectuals who do their best to survive by undertaking the "division of things," they too are "survivors" like the victims whose theory they write. But they are victims of power, certainly in a different way than victims; they are "embedded" at the front or "at the scene of action," as soldiers say. Back turned to power, they will photograph the victims, defer the spectacle, and put "reactions" on hold. One rule alone distinguishes media-embedded intellectuals from humanitarian workers. This is the rule of emergency required by victims. The victim commands imperatively and without pause for verification and reflection; this is the ultimatum of emergency. The victim is nothing or not much, just memory and monument, if it is separated from emergency, from insurrection, from an action that is precisely not a reaction. The media intellectual, like any politician, asks us to be "reactive," but there is nothing but ambiguity in this imperative and in this watchword of emergency . . . . Questions to come: In what way is emergency itself an ultimatum, or what type of emergency creates an ultimatum? In what way is "reactivity" itself in fact a putting on hold? And in what way is the most urgent acting not a re-acting but perhaps a non-acting?

From the victimary to the victimological

We will call overrepresentation or overexposure the type of visibility victims get from mediatic thought, directed

from afar by the spirit of philosophy. We will be care-
ful not to accuse the media too quickly and clumsily
– precisely a specialty of intellectuals – for the media has
become the advance guard of philosophy, the universal medium, even though it specializes in philosophy's
dirty work. This overstatement of transcendence (associations, groups for self-defense that produce political
parties) makes the victim a weapon and an instrument
of vengeance – nationalist, communitarian, geostrategic,
and so forth.

Aside from the last century and a few exceptions, the
victim and the intellectual did not grow up together;
they are not of the same "world," nor perhaps of the
same era. There is a traditional victim, obviously pre-
ceding the media intellectual. This victim is without a
designated intellectual, without an appointed defender;
the tears of the community suffice. This victim was
experienced more or less as immanent or natural (gods,
destiny, war, nature, human maliciousness). But as an
original and foundational value of a new ethical voca-
tion, it is an invention of the twentieth century and one
of its idols, without the anterior causes being able to
be invoked anymore. Related in every instance to an
anonymous, sometimes divine, transcendence (whose
unicity demands sacrifice and legitimates the latter in
the eyes of the victim, who in spite of everything accepts
it), the victim is individuated by this monotheistic, jealous, or elective transcendence. (We could give a Gnostic
reading of Levinas's work: that perhaps in spite of himself, he demonstrates to what extent the victim is God's
hostage, or, more precisely, that God's hostage is his
victim.) The victim's formula is given by common sense
as well as by Levinas: it is the-One-for-the-Other (either

the "very-big" Other, or the "very-unique" Other). The injustice of crime resides in that "for," which must be reinterpreted and transformed.

In every age, every people has mourned its dead, blaming sin, destiny, war – but all this was still part, admittedly in a relative way, of nature as history. In spite of its sense of injustice, did humanity have a "subjective" consciousness of being-victim as a still "natural" process? The victim was immanent, it was "in itself," if we can put it this way, without yet truly existing. But it was, and always is, *individuated by transcendence, by no means by itself*. Without a doubt, the victim – first necessarily natural or religious as much as an object of injustice by definition – begins to ex-ist with the monotheistic disengagement of transcendence. Then, as an *ethical value*, the victim appears with Judaic and Christian sacrificial conditions as well as secularized individualizing (indeed re-paganized) ones. The victim is consummated the first time with the paradigm of Christ, the generic victim, and a second time with the paradigm of the Jew, the particular victim, appearing each time as universal. The victim presupposes an injustice, whether exceptional or natural (for example, climatic), and expands or becomes widespread with the demand for and formation of a specific and more individual right. It is a second immanence, social and juridical, emerging through successive upsurges of transcendence, before perhaps submerging and becoming widespread, for example with the secularization of religions. What remains is the passage to an age of non-theological justice, which would truly be that of the immanence of the generically individuated victim.

When the memory-world, that which remembers

transcendences and gods, takes hold of victims and grows with them, the tide that carries them along swells without ceasing to the point of nausea. Like all values, the victim is not absolutely new, but follows an interest-rate curve and reaches its maximum before dissolving its transcendence in the chaos of the world. As intellectuals have always had a predilection for the victim and correlative abstract values, along with the medias that they need, they accompany this upsurge and settle down on this plateau. Justice, medicine, and psychology take hold of the victim; a science of crime and of the victim, a victimology in search of its threshold of epistemological unblocking is formed parallel to a naturally older criminology; pressure groups form, initially but not exclusively following genocides. They cultivate a memory, which of course turns towards vengeance, then make from it a weapon of demand, of "reparation" and of international compassion. These conditions are also those of the appearance or the accentuation of the intellectual as agent of transcendence who asserts the victim as the relation of the individual and universal values.

These groups and even these intellectuals sometimes claim the title of "survivors." These are the miraculated victims [*victimes miraculées*] who bear witness and take on real victims through representation. They have become "representative," returning from the land of the dead and playing a testimonial role, which is no longer allotted to intellectuals alone. In a way, it is the most direct possible representative democracy of victims. Faced with this daily parade of the dead, compassion becomes nausea, which is also an objective and historical phenomenon. Are intellectuals overactive because of bad conscience, or do they never do enough about it? In any case, the notion is drowned by its vague contours, and must be redefined in a viable concept, which allows not action, but the delimitation of an action that would be only in favor of victims and not their overrepresentation. The problem will be to dissolve the combination, the mix or crossbreeding of victim and intellectual, which works towards the greater glory of the thought-world, and thus towards the production of future victims. It will be a question of conjugating them differently, in a matrix of a scientific nature.

Protesting in the name of truth and courage (yet more overly abstract values), some philosophers call this, in order to fight it, *victimary ideology*, into which some of the scientific motivations of victimology must undoubtedly enter. We will borrow this term from them. But if certain intellectuals lapse into the "victimary," it is because philosophers themselves have already lapsed into victimology. They make of it a unitary conception, confusing the victim's reality with its representation. They wrongly generalize the state of the victim, which as a result actually awakens the very old indifference and sometimes the scorn or the indifference of philosophers for it, their pathos of "strong thought." Inevitable as history itself, yet contradictory, between nature and right, between immanence and transcendence, this victimary ideology is the basis from which we would want to propose another treatment rather than simply rejecting it and thereby risking its return. In any case, it is a symptom of our time: its developments are inevitable, its protests logical. Whatever interpretations are given this phenomenon, what matters is that it forms a symptom and a conjuncture, and a symptom is not judged or condemned, it is dealt with and treated if possible.

The vicious circle of the victim and the intellectual

The first (specifically theoretical) difficulty of victimary ideology, and more profoundly of any victimology, is the choice or the definition of the victim, whose overly general concept lacks "generic" precision. This harmful question emerges from the victimo-logical explosion, not yet that of the victims' rights, but only that of knowing *who* is victim. Who has the right to that title, which all demand and which is in all likelihood usurped? Can we set a criterion of definition or at least of delimitation? History and reflections whose object is the victim do not permit this, so we must proceed otherwise than by media reports and abstraction, by a completely different type of thought, one that is not drawn from the world but from an axiomatization of a portion of these knowledges of the world.

We give the victim a quasi-definition, an "oraxiom," that sets its minimal *but non-sufficient* condition. This is the axiom of the victim's human cause used "negatively." This *generically rather than philosophically universal and necessary* essence is non-sufficient and does not exhaust the victim's occasional givenness. Without this essence, a theory would be impossible. The whole problem is to comprehend what we mean by generic man, this of-the-last-instance essence of humans.

On the contrary, the doxa that common sense and philosophy share presupposes that the victim arises as an ontological proof of misery and suffering; this is the theoretical core of victimology. But to be truly universal as human, that is, generic, the victim must be foreclosed to intellectual Reason and its definitions. For this very reason, it is the victim that will be able to determine the modes of functioning or the decisions of that Reason. It is necessary at least to invert the theoreticist primacy of intellectual Reason over the victim, and rethink what a primacy-without-hierarchy, that is, a prior-priority, is. The victim is the condition that under-determines the intellectual to act without claiming to be able to define or determine who is a victim, being himself manipulated by mediatico-philosophical representation. This is a decisive asymmetry because it breaks the specular circle of the victim and the intellectual. The victim is fore-closed to the discourse and action of the intellectual, but not reciprocally: the intellectual must assume the victim in the victim's own way, in its domain and with its own specific means.

3
The Injustice Done to the Victim

Who has primacy in justice, the criminal or the victim?

Will reparation and mourning be placed at the center of the arrangement [*dispositif*] of justice according to the criminal or the victim? And with humans treated generically, is it still a question of a center and an arrangement? Strange but decisive questions.

Either,[1] as has always been predominantly the case, the criminal is the center and the object of the operation of justice, while punishment and reparation must suffice to objectively ensure the victim's mourning. Consequently, the victim is forgotten; this is its second death, in spite or because of the overrepresentation of the criminal. The victim is twice victim, once as wronged in a criminal act and a second time by efface-ment, albeit legally, of the injury that had been suffered, an effacement whose publicity offends the victim. *Or* we make the victim an essential part of justice, but in order

---

[1] Translators' italics, intended to clarify the syntax.

for it to be efficacious it must be made, in a totally different way, a discrete or vanishing cause, and we must not be tempted to interpret its state as a second death. A new concept, that of the victim's double death or double persecution (symmetrical with the criminal's "double jeopardy" [*double peine*]), must thus be elaborated, along with the means to put an end to it. It seems that in every scenario, it is not only the criminal but also his victim that, in different ways, risks a double jeopardy, a justice of repetition.

Another way of formulating the question, this time in favor of the victim: The machine of justice as a value and an institution – is it a tribunal or an apparatus along the lines of a "matrix"? And Man, can he function as the "center" of an arrangement? Must he reorient or reconstruct the apparatus of rights and laws according to an arrangement principally concerned with transformation rather than punishment or reparation? The institution will not choose but at best will balance (of this much we can be sure) these two aspects. It will assert that punishing the criminal is the only possible reparation, that punishing the criminals allows others "to come to terms" [*faire leur deuil*], as the tele-psychoanalysts say. And, in any case, the solution is not there, in the rather vengeful ideology of financial and memorial reparation, nor in general in the re-establishment of an equilibrium supposed to "give satisfaction to both parties."

Because the victim traditionally does not (except at the center or at least at the outset of the arrangement) place the arrangement of justice under condition, this structural forgetting is the reason the victim must be overrepresented, the object of an ideology that is afraid of forgetting it, and that indulges in an overstatement of slogans and demands. Conversely, in order to put the victim at the outset of the arrangement and give it its true force, we must be willing to in some way efface it or under-represent its cause, to render it discrete, almost vanishing, and thus all the less forgettable, all the more unavoidable for no longer being at the center of an apparatus. It is not a question of replacing judges with victims (nothing would be won by this exchange for personal vengeance), but of seeking in the victim the immanent though non-divine cause of justice. It is according to this paradox of memory and forgetting that the philosophical apparatus, and not only the apparatus of the judicial institution, should be theoretically transformed: it is the very concept of victim as generic, *as Man-in-the-last-instance separated from the subject with which it forms a unilateral complementarity*, that must be re-elaborated, and the concept of the intellectual along with it.

How do we liberate the intellectual and the victim from each other (the one from bad conscience, the other from a second death), liberating them by linking them in a different way than through this system? How do we liberate them from a vicious system where the circuit judges barely postpone spontaneous vengeance and are not sufficiently blind? It is not certain that "blind justice" suffices to "render" justice to victims. In spite of any prejudice of this variety, the victim is not an unfortunate and contingent accident that could be passed off on the necessities of History, hoping for more conciliatory treaties, more classical wars, a more benevolent teleology, less cruel disciplines. The victim implicates Man as being the Real of-the-last-instance and not only as subject and agent. The problem is not to add to this misunderstanding out of the cruelty and stupidity of the history through our institutions, including those of thought, but, with a view to a new knowledge, to subtract from them that which is a priori already subtracted from them and which can thus determine them: Man-in-person.

Double death or continued victimization

It is impossible to treat the victim as an isolated "term," an abstract artifact of the victimological or the juridical triad. In the victimological triad, intellectuals and criminals have privilege as heroes over the victim. They arouse social expression and curiosity, while the victim is decidedly uninteresting and remains unimportant to philosophers or theoretically neglected (sometimes through an excess of memory . . .). According to the conditions of the philosophical structure, the victim's meaning can only appear in its correlation, its opposition, its difference to heroes (of act, of speech, of thought). Beyond its juridical structure as a tribunal, philosophy is the correlation of heroes and victims, more nobly of Immortals and Mortals. Memory as glory is proper to heroes, memory as duty (Judaism) and as work (Christianity) to victims. Whereas heroes are entitled to double glory, ceaselessly reaffirmed (the victory and the celebration of victory or the "triumph"), and sometimes to an "open-air" monumentalization offered to the light, victims are doomed to a double forgetting (death and second death) or to the materiality of written or ritual memory, to a subterranean monumentalization. Victims are the guardians and companions of subterranean gods, buried in the past, without future and without light. They are handed over to a black transcendence, which individuates them poorly and silently, while the heroes are individuated by an idealizing transcendence, solar if not stellar. Of course, when they are not doomed to a profound forgetting and the dishonorable disarray of mass graves, victims sometimes rise to the surface and appear in an inert symbolic writing, a cemetery writing through which they testify, protest, and issue desperate calls to us, calls they know to be mute and to which they are resigned. As for the glory that could fall to them, we know what it is: victims also rise to the surface or to the light, but the poorest, flattest, inglorious light of a television screen. Unlike the philosopher, who begins in the Cave and only plunges back into it after the dazzling sun, the victim is a human, whom the philosopher plunges directly into the Cave, and to whom he never left any chance at all, treating it as an obscure witness to the darkness. The heroes' double glory, and symmetrically, the victims' double death, is programmed by this thought-world, which only operates through doublets.

Two categories of victims marginally interest philosophy. Heretics merit special mention; they are at once criminals, greeted with a haughty condescension after the fact, and victims treated as *in flagrante delicto* or, if you will, "to be tried immediately" before History or the tribunal of the Church. They testify to another humanity and another relation to time; they condense a reputedly impossible humanity, recognizable as generic, in contrast to the victim, which enters into cycles of vengeance and becomes the persecutor in its turn. They are not modalities or variants of the man of Logos; on the contrary, they are the rebellion and even the insurrection-in-person against every totality. As is known, the rejection-penalty for those considered criminals or worse (like traitors who broke the initial pact – whatever it was – and openly refused to affirm its goodness, apostates and renegades from sociodicy and theodicy) is to go unburied or be buried in a land of exile – a double or triple death. In contrast to traditional or mass victims of History, heretics are not even survivors (effective or ideal), and for this reason, they more appropriately suggest the human or a totally different idea of the human. An extreme forgetting, incommensurate with the victims specularly "shown," a memory sufficient only for receiving insult, hate, and slander – this is the ordeal to which they, merciless, lead the imbecility of History.

The second category deserving special mention is that of survivors and their unease. The modern victim adds an additional twist to the victim's traditional form. It presupposes a new experience of Man, as Survivor damaged by a continued death, affected by an interminable dying. In general, modern man is thought as shaped, damaged, seamed by death, the death of Others and therefore his own. The death of Others belongs, in varying degrees, to his vacillating identity. The Survivor should also in all probability have died; in a certain sense he is dead, but "he came through" de facto or *de jure*. He is "miraculated," and from the bottom of his heart he can thank transcendence and its miracles, certain of which could very well be pure philosophical miracles. The Survivor is defined by the death of Others-that-I-am ("the days of our death"). Such is the cogito of the Survivor: as Other I am dead thus I [*je*] survive not only as a diminished or reduced I [*Moi*], but also as a miraculated I [*Moi*]. This I is thus structured as an Other, as modern philosophy postulates it, and even by the Other, as contemporary philosophy postulates it. It is divisible and divided, and survives outside of the self, in the memory of itself that it was as Other and therefore as the Other of the Other.

In the thought-world, the being of man is a unity woven of relations; his life is a syndrome of permanent threat, which makes a multiplication of death, a continued death, possible. But already the Soul of the Greeks responded to a problem of survival, and immortality is still formulated in this way today by common sense and the majority of religions, in the terms of survival. "Resurrection" will provide a corrective to this conception. It is one of philosophy's customary paradoxes to call "sur-vival" [*sur-vie*] that which would seem to be rather an "under-life" [*sous-vie*]. Indeed, the one does not come without the other, and always for the benefit of the one representing superiority and glory.

Precisely in the tradition of the philosophical triad, the criminal and the intellectual have more prestige than the victim. The intellectual is certainly a smaller-scale philosopher, but a philosopher nonetheless, and thus virtually a hero of thought, while the victim is instead neglected or forgotten (the present chatter changing nothing in the matter or even confirming it). Consequently, in philosophy, as well as in law and justice, there is misfortune for the defeated. The victim rarely or never has the tribute of glory; one owes it the tribute of memory, one concedes courage to it, sometimes the spirit of sacrifice, but in the grave the victim loses its singularity, its individuality, and passes into the grayish and stony generalities of memory. Undoubtedly the victim is too silent for the philosophers, those men of speech; that is the problem, and it is the victim's silence that must be interpreted by identifying it in a repeated mediatic display. By definition, the victim lets out at most a *Why? Why me? Why us?* wholly incapable of making Logos in the manner of Plato at Socrates' deathbed ... Plato is perhaps the first intellectual to find "his" victim, to make himself its defender, but already in the figure of an idealized hero, "fallen" for the honor of Truth. Every hero is one day "fallen," but there are those who in spite of everything remain upright, and those who plunge into forgetting. Like the Greek temple whose opening Heidegger celebrates, the Hero tears himself from the earth and continues opening a world. *The victim opens no new world, but closes the old ones.* This suffocated speech, on the edge of extinction, unleashes (just after a time of surprise rather than a time of respect) the discourse of survivors and the din of culpability in others, perhaps the background noise that occupies Logos.

By way of an ethics, we would readily call not for respect but for a certain *imitation of the silence of victims.* This does not mean falling absolutely silent or giving ourselves over to the gesticulations of a bad, loud mimeticism ("We are all victims," "all German Jews," etc.), but *making a use-of-silence of and with that philosophical speech to which intellectuals are moreover compelled.* Certainly, we must honor victims with memory at least the way we honor their deaths. But memory, like work, is an argument for the benefit of the worker of memory, who hands the victim over to philosophical capital (which serves us as thought) and wrenches the victim away from itself a second time. As for memory as duty, it finally delivers the victim over to a divine and exacting transcendence. It is the ultimate sacrifice, another form of its second death.

This is the problem upon which philosophy, as a

two-faced form of the world, founders – as there is double jeopardy for criminals and double glory for heroes, philosophy calls for or tolerates a double death for victims. Understood as an animal of reason, the city, or religion, man seemingly must be killed twice. To finish him off, that is, to immortalize him indefinitely, our system of thought necessarily takes him up two times. We also ask ourselves "Why?" Why – for what overly sufficient reason – send the victim to a protracted death rather than to death once each time, exterminating it a second time through concept, meaning, or a jealous (indeed, a cruel and stupid) God? As always, thought surrenders and hands victims over to the doublets it proliferates. In memory as piety or as an imperative, we cannot find a solution that would free victims from the tomb of thought, from its monumentalization. Behind these Christian and Judaic solutions, mixed with theological usage, only the figure of the survivor is distinguished, doubtless a noble figure but not as innocent as that of the victim. For the victim, is it a question of surviving outside of the self, in the memory and the goodwill of survivors who we supposedly would also be? How would a universal survival be possible if there is no life to support it, or better than a life, a lived experience that would be without-life and thus without-death, and that would be the prior-to-the-first or "last" condition of human acting and human resurrection? In the generic victim, we discover not a new doublet but a unique power, which afterwards, but only afterwards, is divided into its object and its occasion, the crime. This unique power, revived but not repeated, is capable of disclosing in a single immanent lived experience that a crime took place, that is, that there is indeed a criminal, and of denouncing the crime, not only manifesting it but resisting it on principle. It is really this philosophical aporia that must be explained in order to put an end to the division of labor between the intellectual and the victim, so that a single superposed lived experience suffices to undergo oppression and be the force capable of liberating itself from that oppression. Intellectuals will wait, not victims. If the human was made in the image of God, why couldn't he be made even more so, and for "ontological" reasons, in the image of the victim, the object par excellence of victimization? We will have understood that it is impossible to leave to Judaism the title role or the classic example of victim. It is undoubtedly necessary that humans taken as a generic body be the of-the-last-instance cause that offers individuals (alone or en masse) up to victimization while denouncing it through their uprising or making that victimization visible to intellectuals.

Victims and the intellectuals' betrayal

To intellectuals one will make the same very general objection that certain Gnostics make to the Judaic God, and which we generically extend to every theology: that their intervention is unsuccessful and testifies to a certain "objective" insufficiency that is satisfied with an unconscious persecutorial will. More modestly, we will speak of a lack of inventiveness, which is another thing altogether from ontological wandering or being taken hostage, even if it ends in jealous surveillance. We will not contrast a betrayal of the betrayal to the betrayal of the victim by intellectuals, who, by submission to the thought-world, have overlooked the victim's radical humanity and contributed to its infinite persecution. The only response is a priori yet real, *still before* the betrayal, a prior-to-the-first defense of victims. We define Man or Victim as the Inverse-in-person [*l'Envers-en-personne*] of the intellectuals, as the radical immanence that by means of unilaterality passes through the inversion those intellectuals carry out. Debasing transcendence and its all-powerfulness, Man-in-person inverts the priorities and thus the hierarchy of Good and of Evil by ordering creation (supposedly good, but in fact a failure) according to the inmost misfortune that constitutes humans.

The uncomfortable situation of intellectuals is resolved by permanent betrayal. How would they not be twisting and turning in the winds of the event [*à tous les vents de l'événement*], caught as they are between, on the one hand, abstract values without a grounding in reality (to which they are affixed like a nail or a pivot) and, on the other, the turnstile of History, which they are obliged to follow, so great is their anxiety at missing it and so restrictive their mediatic and dramatic greed. Their identification with these universal values – in reality philosophico-worldly values – constrains them to take part, side, and position in the great game of History, which does not cease to buffet them from one side to the other. But can we cease to take sides or positions without sinking into quietism? That seems strictly impossible in the most general philosophical context. We do not need a new stoicism or ataraxia, but a complete change in the paradigm of thought for which existing philosophies would be nothing more than empirical models of interpretation under the conditions of the world. What kind of thought do we need? An a priori thought that is, however, woven into the real of Man, therefore made of axioms that are concrete in-the-last-instance, of oraxioms lived or "material" like him. These axioms of a new sort institute relations-without-relation, "non-relations" with victims. There is no gentle or measured solution to the intellectual betrayal of victims, no remedy for a constitutive gesture, only perhaps the greatest possible betrayal, in the form of a defensive ultimatum.

But how to take up the world or History non-philosophically, as a kind of error or disaster of an unknown type, misrecognized by philosophy – philosophy, which has made a mission and a highly prized specialty of the assumption of the world and of History? With the world as specular and hallucinatory duplicity, it is no longer a question of "original sin," but perhaps of an ante-theological "original divine sin." Is this the creation of an insufficient or malicious God, or rather of a thought – philosophy – too shrewd and sly? It is not, in any case, the work of a supposedly good God; it is rather a specular magic in which their relations develop. Seemingly created by a deceitful God or a God who did not have the means to fulfill his ambition, philosophy misleads intellectuals after the manner of philosophers who work "spontane-ously." But the more fundamental problem is that of its cause, if there is one, as philosophy or form-world. Why talk about "original error" when it is a question of phi-losophy's very existence, not its historical existence but its being and its effects? These two terms ought to be cor-rected according to this cause.

Only the one who comes to the victim's aid not by prolonging its agony but by codetermining without delay and reviving simultaneously its manifestation of crime and its power to mobilize its resistance can take on the victim. What is necessary here is what we have called compassion as the revival of the acting of non-acting proper to the victim. The *In-person* turned intellectual is what ensures a priori the only salvation the victim tolerates. The thrownness [*L'être-jeté*] of Man, *for* the form of the world rather than *towards* its "facticity" (Heidegger), is obviously not itself the positive cause of this Evil-world – that would be to return to a theology of the Devil – but only its negative condition of salvation or of the glorification of his Identity-in-person. So much so that the ability to liberate oneself does not nullify but is already a destiny and a misfortune – that of human solitude before the world – which are asserted in that liberation. But to betray in this way the world and History, which are betrayal itself, as Man-in-person does – is that still a betrayal? Faithfulness is neither betraying betrayal nor making war on war (intellectuals can do nothing but take pleasure, despite everything, in this sort of dialectical circle), but being taken up as Man threatened with betrayal by philosophy, who has already responded a priori with the force of his Identity, obliging the world to make itself suitable for victims. Only Man-in-person, not the Intellectual given over to the world, is capable of this Identity, which turns betrayal against "itself." To return to our initial problem: having its cause in the ultimate In-person allows for the transformation of the Evil-world, its anonymous and ontological facticity, the removal of its "original" mythological and theological nature from it and the recognition in it of its more than originary, "generic" feature. And it will be unbelievable that what appears as a simple flaw or a lack of inventiveness in the relation to the world is a superficial affect

– this lack of inventiveness in resistance is tragic, however immanent it may also be to humans.

The victim is the Inverse-in-person or the last-instance of intellectuals and, furthermore, of philosophers. Because it is in any case impossible to betray the victim actually and definitively, they have in reality betrayed only the subject, as one might expect, but they do not cease to antithetically believe either that they did not betray it or that they could betray it. This antithetical is a shared belief and their true betrayal. Concretely, the intellectuals' values of justice (even rights of man) have their own "value," which is no longer a value because it determines, but in-the-last-instance, all valuation. To what extent does man introduce justice into the world? Formulated generally in this way, the question demands a moral and circular response, but Man-in-person is the Just-without-justification that determines the unjust justice that is the world.

If it is still believed that the economic or theological truth of ethics is reparation in this world or the next, it is urgent to invert this hierarchical structure of justice based on a human Identity-in-person. Inversion is here a radical but not absolute gesture, an Inverse foreclosed to the Absolute. As for the duality of transcendentals that traces the circle of ethics, the hierarchy of Good and Evil, it would be a mistake to be content with overturning it and to stand "beyond" (Nietzsche) without appealing to an immanence of superposition. Its *inversion*, which is to say the *hierarchical primacy of Evil (or of not-Good) over Good*, is only tolerable by a mutation of transcendent Evil as it is imagined by religions and philosophies. But as has been said, this not-Good is necessary to the Good, which itself is not "sufficient" to completely exhaust the ethical real. If now there is a *priority of "Evil" included in the prior-priority of Good*, it can no longer be a mythological entity stemming from religious aberrations, but the solitude or radical misfortune of the in-person human Identity insofar as they hand it over to and predestine it for the world and its duplicity. It is not a question of denying, pure and simple, the world, which is the correlate (the "uni-late") of Man, or rather of denying their complementarity, but of giving oneself the means of preventing oneself from being indefinitely and absolutely enclosed in the world, that is, in its magic. A simple overturning of Good and Evil would only further muddle the confusions introduced by religions into ethics, multiplying duplicity by itself. It is philosophy that is moral through its duplicity, not Man who himself is the last non-moral instance of all ethics. Man is calm Identity, the non-acting that has the force to *pour* philosophical and religious ethics out of its duplicity, its lies, and its art of exceptions. He pours the world out of itself without totally suppressing it as in a process of destruction, leaving it instead transformed by and for the subject. It is within this framework that the struggle against the "persecutorial victims" that we always are in History must be formulated.

The concept of vectorial or "weak force"[2]

We formulate two axioms intended to explain the "a priori defense" of victims. The first, which we have

---

[2] Throughout this section, we render the French *force* as force. The reader should keep in mind that it also denotes *strength*, and is frequently contrasted with *faiblesse,* or weakness. [*Trans.*]

already mentioned, is the type of a priori body or mate-riality that is liable in victims to be opposed to the body of persecutors and sometimes of survivors. The second concerns the type of force and weakness that belongs to Man-in-person and thus to victims. These two concepts, "glorious body" and "weak force," can be introduced into ethics to explain the possibility of persecution and the other possibility, that of the struggle against persecution.

The dualysis [*dualyse*] of the unitary concept of "force," in the form of a unilateral complementarity, distinguishes "weak force" from any blending and attributes it to Man-in-person as victim, and "strong force" or excessive "force-of-force," attributing it to philosophy and its modalities. Weak force is specific and qualitative (generic), and not a strong force weakened. Its essence is radical weakness or the acting of its non-acting, that by which it struggles against strong force and its duplicity.

We know the recent oppositions of "weak thought" and "strong thought." This sort of massive duality, which amounts to going round in circles, limits the imag-ination. One of Nietzsche's paradoxes is well known but certainly subtler: *the strong need to be protected from the weak*. It is Platonizing and pushes a sophistic thesis to its limit, ascribing to the truly strong – strong in essence or in life – the need to be defended against the accumulated and sly force of the "weak," who yearn for vengeance by means of intelligence. Force and weak-ness have lost their simply quantitative character and have acquired a qualitative and ontological character, but the cunning of the weak is precisely to (re)quantify their weakness and to transform it into an insidious force destructive of the heroes of civilization. The strong thus need a qualitative supplement of force – the will to affirmative power – to fight against the truly weak. In this dialectic of quantity and quality reside the overturnings of the qualitative into the quantitative, arranged in a unitary and continuous manner despite moving to a difference of quality. Force retains its traditional philosophical primacy, which it might need for protection. Philosophy's torsions are necessary to understand that force must be defended and that the strong can be victims, that force and weakness are divided, shared, and combined in a way that is not quantitative.

The totality of philosophical presuppositions is involved in the thesis of the ontico-ontological primacy of force. It is useless to simply substitute weakness for it, endowing weakness with the same sort of primacy and priority, even if weakness has something inalienable about it that it does not owe to force as the philosophical *agon* always postulates. Therefore, its defense *as weakness and not as lesser force* only seems necessary when it – radical weakness by definition or by axiom – falls of its own essence outside of the balance of power [*rapports de force*] and *acts under certain "complementary" or "occasional" conditions that make weakness a subject in the grip of the adverse forces of the world*. For its part, force would instead be the means of defense of that weakness. We thus support an axiom that distributes force and weakness in a way that is not unitary and blended. It is weakness as the radical absence of full force (or of force-of-force – here a complete analysis of the redoubling of force would be necessary) that is the real and possesses the prior-priority of the real. But the radical absence of force does not signify absolute absence, only that weakness is "in-person" through radical immanence or superposition, empty for its part of all unitary notions of force and all blending with it. This emptiness [*vide*] cannot just be passively endured despite its essential weakness; it is this weakness that "creates a vacuum" [*fait le vide*] around itself, an emptiness that is never absolute. Radical weakness must possess, and precisely as weakness, a certain proper or lived force in-person – this is the "vectorial" insurrection. Our axiom is this, and we contrast it with Nietzsche's: *weakness contains a vector, a "weak force" by which it defends itself "without force" against the strong force that it under-determines.*

This notion of "weak force" must be explained. Strong force is the foundation of philosophy, the force-of-force or its auto-affirmation. Weak force is simple in its state of superposition of vectors and enjoys a relative autonomy proper to radical weakness. Weakness, as radical immanence, is the essence of force as "weak force" and opposes strong force. The weakness of the Victim-in-person thus shares nothing with any force of the world whatsoever, and yet it is not without force even though it shares nothing with it. For its part, force – that of language for example – is not an autonomous entity such as one normally finds in the world or in History. Force adds nothing real to generic weakness. By contrast, it partakes of weakness. Weakness and force must be thought not together – for fear of an infinite dialectical paradox – but unilaterally and complementarily, each as weakness in-the-last-instance, even language, even force. What then is this weak force that accompanies weakness-in-person? It is not a weakened, damaged, degraded – which is to say divided – force. Philosophy is not at all equipped to think these types of concepts, invented by physics and formalized here generically. Philosophy thinks too much according to the bad crossbreeding of blending to recognize their autonomy, which is qualitative and proper to that which for philosophy is only nuances or degrees. As a vector, weak force is a full or indivisible force and, because of this indivisibility, it is radical weakness and mechanical non-acting. Participation is possible without confusion – non-Platonic participation that is resolved by the being-separated or foreclosed of vectorial immanence or radical weakness. We therefore distinguish between "force-of-force," supposedly in and for itself, the way philosophy and the exteriority of transcendence hallucinates it; "force-in-person," or weak force, insofar as it belongs to the non-sufficiency of Man or of the victim; and finally, "force (of) thought," which belongs to the subject and whose essence is the former.

From the Victim-in-person to the ecology of the survivor

Whether anonymous or monumentalized in memory, the victim – such at least as the world understands and captures it – is reduced to a continuous process of victimization. Once the always poorly crossed boundary of passing away is traversed – the aporetic and poorly defined instant of "death," which the Greeks greatly simplified and falsified in their will to wisdom (imagining death in the form of sleep or of rupture) – the victim survives at the edge of the living, giving them a funereal depth, as if the victim hesitated or had trouble dying, refused by nothingness and life alike, eternalizing the aporia of life and death – another way of being set up in the world as if on an interface and of inhabiting it with the blessing of the sky and in the anguish of burial. Humanity carefully accumulates capital meant to assure its survival. And yet, philosophy, which collects all the features of survival and capital together, also belongs to the same sort of activity. It consummates itself by wallowing or persecuting itself, accumulating its dead, those that it produces and saves as treasure. It is a two-faced capital, a dark side turned towards the earth where it survives as the exploitation of memory's reserves, and a light side turned towards Logos, in which it does not cease to reproduce, extorting a surplus value from its workers. Of philosophy as capital, one sees in general only the luminous side, the one that it produces and reproduces as its sky. Even so, philosophy has not one but two theologies, not one but two fetishisms – one of the sky, the other of the earth. The dead also carry on underground traffic: their economy is insatiable and they form a black capital accumulated in the undergrounds of real transcendence, symmetrical to the theological capital accumulated in the celestial realms of ideality. One recognizes philosophy's duplicity, its double transcendence, the doublet with which it severs humans.

A more human conception would link victims to their generic being rather than to their philosophical memory. This is the axiom said of Man-in-person or of the glorious body. It permits the laying down of a complementarity that unilaterally associates the Victim-in-person and the individual subject, instead of a doublet that forces them to mirror each other. This complementarity is that of a generic being-victim, which explains the necessary but non-sufficient possibility for humans alone to be intimately given not to the situation but to the occasion of victimization. Only they, in a certain way, that is, in-the-last-instance, assume the paradigmatic function of the victim, even if they are not the only victims. For obviously the state of the victim extends far beyond humans, but it is only because there are humans that there are in-the-last-instance other victims that must share the fate of the generic species. Everything is not equalized in the name of universal life or the universal will-to-live, the way Schopenhauer's Hindu thought equalizes everything in the name of suffering, or in the name of a species condemned to disappear for ecological reasons. The introduction of the ecological and biological parameter into this problem requires the extension of the notion of victim beyond any anthropology and anthropocentrism; but ecology and anthropology alike remain natural and positive givens, and it is certainly not on this specific and "factual" plane that we place the Victim-in-person itself, but on the generic plane. For the Victim-in-person is that which, like every "victim" of an occasion, has an obscure and unreflective knowledge [*savoir*] of that occasion, but which can above all acquire the recognition [*connaissance*] of that state and the power to resist it. One will object that this re-establishes the old humanist priority; but it is nothing of the sort if at least we know that humans establish a non-commutative, non-reversible order between themselves and the rest of "creation," an order of the prior-to-the-first Last Instance rather than of priority and of hierarchy. The all-victims haunting philosophy and certain sectarian apocalypses, without mentioning original sin, is the best way to render all resistance impossible. It is the rather diabolical work of the world, one that makes the miracle of divine salvation necessary.

Measured according to this complex generic criterion, ecological and biological victims are victims by default, so to speak, by lacking the power of resistance. In any case, they are victims of an act of war and devastation, to which humanity leads itself. Of them one can say that they are doubly victims, perhaps even more so than humans since the knowledge of their situation hardly grants them the power to resist. Conversely, humans are responsible for helping "non-generic" species whether it is possible or not, but this will always indirectly benefit them, because they are *also* a species.

The two superposed rivers of life and death

Thus, the Victim-in-person is not a survivor, the numb I of an Other, even if it can give that impression in the confusion of the real and reality. Even at the worst of its degradations, it remains the glorious body that it is before being consigned to survival. What does this being-glorious of man untouched by "his" death mean? Undoubtedly, we have the feeling of being immortal, but it is not really a matter of Spinoza's conception, which also entrusts individual immortality to a substance (of immanence, but) transcendent and divine. Being-glorious maintains the wholeness of its identity in-person, its incessantly revived being of superposed lived experiences. Its radical immanence is not achieved through the convergence or gathering of the memory of others around an imaginary transcendent center or through a collective or communitarian ego, but rather through the interference of their lived-experiences-without-ego.

It is an equally material and vectorial lived experience, an insistent rather than a consistent materiality, a neutral and non-subjective mobility. This lived experience is indivisible, although, unlike the soul, susceptible to addition; it is a "mystical" body, an undulatory phenomenon in a "complex" or "imaginary" dimension, which does not cease to elude religion or, in any case, theology. It is by their lived materiality that humans, whether real victims or not, form a wave of immanence for the rest of creation. The glorious body is the point of collision or interference of the two rivers, which philosophy always distinguishes in order to re-blend them a bit further along, that of life and that of death, without managing to make a unique wave. Is life that which resists death or the same river as death, like two rivers that do not cease to engulf or envelop each other? An insoluble question because it is philosophical and guided by macroscopic schemas. It is necessary to displace this antinomy with a generic lived experience, immanent by interference and capable of modeling a non-mechanical collision of life and death, of under-determining what the simple blends of life–death contain that is victimizing, and of displacing them from their sufficient state as doublets. Death and life are in a state of superposition and not of blending, so much so that death does not traverse the immanence of the glorious body. It is this immanence that traverses the transcendence of gods, of God, of life as well as death that operates in the world.

As phenomenal or real content, as the insistent lived experience in the victim, Man-in-person cannot be buried, either in the earth or in the sky; only the individual subject as its "remains" can be. It does not itself exist as a subject stripped of its attributes by an external accident. It insists as stripped in-prior-priority, and defends itself in this way against death, which seeks it out, and against life, which harasses it but which cannot absolutely strip it of its predicates because it already lost that absolute predicate, the All. If the subject as stripped lives on in the earth, in monument, writing, and rite, the Victim-in-person on the contrary insists (indeed, "in-sists") in the No Where, in the "Not-Where" (Suhrawardi), and, we will add, in the "Not-When." Man is not reducible to a subject and its relations; there are no generic human *relations*, traces, or trajectories to mark or punctuate them, but rather, on the one hand, the inhuman as well as human mixtures – impassable as such in their equivocity – and on the other hand, their coming-under, determined in-the-last-instance as humans-without-mixture. The generic provides no purity (purity is the dream of mixtures), but this intimate nudity can act and topple all transcendences, those of the earth and of the sky, into a more radical immanence. The problem is thus not to be immortal through a kind of simple opposition of immortal life to death, but to not have to die or live twice. The problem is of a lived experience under-determining the life-world. To die and to live once each time like a transfinite being, this is the sign of our Humanity and of what in it exceeds or determines the subject. From the point of view of the world, the subject can die and perhaps live several times, but Man dies as subject one single time each time. This is its non-biological immortality, its immanent being-lived insofar as it vectorially comes-under the subject. There is a way in which each victim of an injustice has been or will be by its memory a persecutorial and thus a sufficient victim. It is difficult and almost impious to speak of a sufficiency of victims, in particular universal victims of life, which all the dead are. They cannot be justified, their sufficiency erased, except as generic.

4
Deduction of Murder and Persecution

Mechanism of the generic matrix

Given the formalism required here by a general theory of victims, we pass over many significant and necessary nuances in silence, not distinguishing, for example, between murder and persecution-as-double-persecution. We do not make crime a thing-like and cynical – nor simply a juridical – idea. Crime, too, is a concept, the criminal a subject; but both have a generic sense, which must be made the object of theory and knowledge. This generic mechanism needs to be elucidated.

There is no perfect symmetry or antinomy between hero and victim. Let us remember that the hero enjoys an idealizing and specular glory as well as speech with a minimum of immanence; the victim sinks into the material immanence of the body and the earth, as well as that of writing, and acquires a certain transcendence without redoubling, a simple and obscure ideality. Against Greek pathos, without reaching Judaic pathos, we have posed Man on the side of the victim "instead" of that of the hero, and we situate the victim according to Man-in-person as glorious body and weak force. Man-in-person can obviously find its fulfillment in the over-human or be sublimated in the hero, but it is first of all as such that it is the negative or non-sufficient cause of the victim and can be extended to the rest of creation for which it is responsible. We carry out an incarnate inversion of the old domination of the hero over the victim. We formulate Man-in-person and its primacy as the Inverse-in-person of this hierarchy, and from it we deduce the first destination of the subject as victim rather than hero.

To make the matter intelligible, we need a matrix, with its duality of places or variables. Only it can conjugate the two individuals, the criminal and the victim, and decide on their relative weight and the nature of their relation. At first glance, everything happens between individual subjects (in a general sense), but this between-subjects, if it seems to be actual and determined by the world, is also virtually under-determined as generic. If we take into account the double possible version of the same generic mechanism according to one or the other protagonist, the crime and the victim are thinkable in a single process, though not as "the same." There is crime when the process of the matrix is thought, that is, practiced as well, from the point of view of the world or of philosophy, when this mechanism is in the end "interpreted" by worldly causes. This is the interpretation according to the criminal, or even according to the judge, who assumes the same sort of objectivity as the criminal even if he condemns the facts. But when the matrix is interpreted in prior-priority by the victim and no longer by the criminal, the crime appears with a completely different meaning, as *crime in-the-last-instance against man or as victimization.* In other words, the victim is an interpellated individual subject insofar as it is a subject through other subjects (as a cause that is, in any case, occasional), but it is more deeply interpellated as the glorious body it takes on or as a materiality a priori able to suffer or rejoice, to be an affected body. As such it is exposed, exceedingly weak although resistant; it possesses the "double" power of the victim. The victim immediately proves its human reality or its being-real, whereas the hero dissolves them in ideality. Its materiality is demonstrated in its defeat, in its being-defeated. The insistent or virtual weakness of Man makes the conquering violence of subjects given over to the world possible and effective, so much so that Man-in-person is not a rational animal – still a benedictory definition for the glory of God – but rather the "animal" most persecuted by man himself under the influence of the attraction of the world. It is precisely because it is not in its essence a simple animal, even a "rational" animal, that it is persecutable in-the-last-instance. That is a necessity – doubtless non-sufficient – of persecution. Persecution is conditioned by the a priori being-persecutable that makes up humans, but is also occasioned by the world, that is, by philosophy which is its form. "Man is a wolf to man" is the philosophical and reversible version of our formula, another way of interpreting the situation from the point of view of the wolf-philosophers.

The cause of crime, an immanental appearance

Therefore, one kills a subject, that is, a set of worldly relations, in-the-last-instance or in-prior-priority because it is a Man-in-person condemned not to react or to act without reflexively reacting. As a non-sufficient condition of possibility, the In-person allows this confusion with the subject, which it assumes and numbs. Its status explains the possibility of persecution, real for the subject, hallucinatory for Man-in-person. Precisely because it is human, the victim can defend itself a priori, and here "a priori" does not mean self-defense – quite to the contrary. Persecuting the subject while using as an excuse the victim's weakness or non-acting, which is a negative cause of persecution unknown to the world itself, the world believes, hallucinating, that it persecutes or destroys Man, not knowing that he is an *inalienable* weakness. The criminal transforms what was the non-sufficient cause of persecution into a sufficient reason for his act. He is himself a victim of hallucination regarding his victim. Thus, continued victimization is death reflected by the world or philosophy, the redoubled death of the subject confused with Man-in-person, hounding it with a more than "transcendental" illusion proper to the criminal. Persecution comes more specifically from the confusion of the means or the productive forces humans have at their disposal and the transcendent or worldly finalities according to which they organize those means. The same means that could help humans become ambiguous as soon as these finalities take charge of them. That which could struggle against persecution is put in its service. It is a hijacking of the generic by the philosophical capital that makes up the world.

In this way, it is possible to immanently but non-sufficiently deduce crime and the resistance to crime. We do not affirm that *all* men (if such a thing exists or can still be formulated) are victims and/or criminals, a statement made possible by victimary ideology or the ideology of the survivor. That would be a return to philosophy and its confusions. We are spontaneous criminals and persecutors condemned to be able to actually become so because we are *in-the-last-instance* victims, and this for the very same reason: our humanity. Indeed, humanity's simplicity, *while remaining itself right to the end*, takes on two destinies as soon as it encounters the world. Thus, we are no longer these two things, persecutors and persecuted, in a manner rendered circular and reversible by vengeance, exchanging our predicates or circulating them between us. We are not *all and always* this way. In fact, it is being victims that lets us escape from the law of "all" or of the countable. It is as humans-in-person that we are in-the-last-instance criminals who have eluded the law of the world due to their status as victims.

We have thus made a different hypothesis from that of the survivor. This one distinguishes the generic human as radically indivisible from the subject it under-determines, but which is given as divisible from the outset. Their duality is unilateral: the subject has Man for its condition, rather than presupposing him, whereas Man presupposes the subject and its relations to the world only occasionally. In this hypothesis, it is understood that it is the subject who is victim, not Man-in-person, even though it is the subject's necessary but non-sufficient condition and a priori material form. Here is in fact the principle of what will be the "resurrection:" Man-in-person or the glorious lived experience is the negative condition of death, of the subject, but it itself does not die when the subject dies. It is the weakness or the without-force, the non-acting that makes up Man. Philosophical arrogance was ignorant of this, confusing his weakness in existence with an unassuming figure, subject to an operation of vanishing or to a limit-trace.

A double causality, or rather a unilateral duality of cause and occasion, is therefore necessary to understand persecution and victimization. A man is persecuted for a reason (his ideas, his "race," his action), which the persecutor uses to sorrowfully rationalize his undertaking. If there is a cause of this sort, it is not only a facade or dissimulation for deeper mechanisms (economic, ideological, religious, etc.), but it is "ontologically" second, a necessary but occasional cause. However, to really explain persecution, to explain it better than a priori, in prior-priority in the sense of the "real" such as we understand it, there must be much more than an occasion. A cause is necessary though non-sufficient: Man-in-person, *which is thus never the subject of persecution or its direct object, but its non-sufficient cause or cause of-the-last-instance.* There is the glorious body "behind" or "in" the crime, but as immanent – deeper and more given than any hidden mechanism. It is its negative possibility and not at all the direct stakes of the struggle that sets subjects at odds. Not only is it uncertain that one persecutes pure ideas or even supposedly racial features in their abstraction, but indeed it is more likely that it is their bearers or their quasi-material supports, their generic materiality, that furnish a supposedly sufficient reason for murder.

Immanent but non-sufficient deduction of crime

How could Man-in-person in its weakness, Man-in person that is non-sufficiency itself, provide a sufficient reason for persecution? If Man-in-person itself is not such a positively acting and fully necessary reason, if it is nothing but a Last Instance, it is the desire that subjects in-the-world experience for it that leads them to believe that Man-in-person is this sufficient reason leading them to crime. This is the hallucination of subjects claiming to identify with Man, to subvert their unilateral complementarity, and to interpret the non-sufficient cause precisely as the sufficient reason for persecution. Subjects in the system of the world can only persecute others, themselves, insofar as they are *ultimately* humans, an ultimacy that also indicates that they need an occasion or external motivation to offset this lack of necessity. They are reduced to their ideas, their culture, their history, or their physical characteristics; they give to other subjects (that is, also to themselves) a figure, while as humans these are invisible or in-person identities, at worst subjects-strangers. Insofar as they are enchanted and informed by the world, they cannot but want to identify with Man; in a hallucinatory way they desire the real, which they are anyway, albeit in a non-sufficient manner. One cannot want to kill except through this kind of murderous identification, which is the overturning of human causality of-the-last-instance and its transformation into a specular image of the subject. And as human identity cannot be found – the vanished-without-vanishing, reduced to the figure of the Stranger – identification with this identity is unfinished and interminable. Thus arises the necessity to pursue murder and to "finish" what is by definition in-the-last-instance unfinishable. The terrifying and universal pursuit of persecution, and more commonly of death, by each of the subjects-in-the-world that we are comes from the fact that, wishing to identify himself with Man but being unable to do so directly, the murderer hounds his subject, representing it so as to (not) finish with it. The persecutor is the object of a confusion we will call "immanental" according to its most distant and last condition, and not transcendental or limited and produced under philosophical conditions. Philosophy takes part in that hunting of Man-in-person from the first row, and perhaps even leads it. Nietzsche denounced the lying priest behind the philosopher, but perhaps it is a criminal who advances masked behind the names of Being, Consciousness, Spirit, Absolute Knowledge, and other fetishes. Not that philosophy doesn't have at its disposal prohibitions and safeguards, its "humanism," but these are fragile, founded on the misrecognition of the real danger which comes from its deepest core.

If being a victim is a possibility for which Man must be considered as uncovered "in-person" in his very invisibility, that is as a subject-Stranger, and where the world tries to profit from his being-uncovered, can we not draw the consequence that it is necessary and lawful to kill or persecute humans without further ado? There is persecution if a Persecuted-without-persecution (or an Arisen-without-resurrection) – to take up again this sort of formula by unilateral subtraction – is already virtually given before any real persecution. It is a necessary condition, but it presupposes the addition of the operation of persecution. "Sufficiency" occurs or makes us believe that it occurs with natural and historical causes that strike the subject in actuality [*effectivité*] by which Man exists in-the-world. Intellectuals are not in fact interested in anything except this "How?," which comes too late, at the ethical limitation or the a posteriori judgment of the committed act. But the "Why?" presumes that persecution ought to be distinguished, in and through the Persecuted, from animal conflict, from natural, biological, or social struggle, if it hopes to be recognized [*reconnue*] and above all known [*connue*] as human. Philosophy postulates that killing a man is possible, sometimes necessary or inevitable, and that the only thing to be done, since it makes all these modalities continuous, is to limit this continuity by cuts. It is an ontological reasoning, which can be applied as vainly to a murderous subject as to a good and all-powerful God. We do not make this vicious assumption, which leads as always to an ethics of limitation and the border. To kill the subject, or Man only insofar as he *exists* at grips with the world, is possible without being sufficient or necessitating, and only becomes necessary under various additional conditions. But we must also admit that confusion is possible and sufficient (only from the point of view of the world) for persecutors due to this precarity of Man-in-person, which only receives (non-empirical or philosophical) existence in and through the subject. Put differently, there is a principle of the victim's non-sufficiency to be persecuted insofar as it is individual: the victim *ultimately demands to be persecuted* a priori *but in a non-sufficient or non-necessitating way*, just as it ultimately but not categorically demands to be defended not by "somebody else" but by the human that it is. The intersubjectivity of subjects, which is nothing but a factual in-the-world norm, must be discarded from the problematic and replaced by the *imperative and contingent demand* that, as Man-in-person, I am also the fragile Other or the subject-Stranger.

The victim is without a doubt in-the-last-instance

Man as non-acting facing philosophico-worldly sufficiency, which claims to appropriate it and is ready
to believe that the victim "feigns," if one can say that,
weakness or non-acting, which seems for its part "to
call for" the desire of identification and the pretension
of the world. *Human or subjectless non-acting is thus
the supreme trap for philosophy, which is the world
desiring to legislate the human real.* As non-acting, Man
is the victimizable par excellence, which "motivates" a
general, innocent, and natural violence. But the victim is
the only weak force capable of forcing the world, rather
than such an event. Man-in-person can force the world
to change, but the world, however, can only force the
subject, and not Man, who is too weak and the basis of
the subject.

This is an attempt at an immanent but without sufficient reason deduction of crime, of its possibility, and
even of its reality, beginning from the moment one
accepts that there is always an occasional cause as well.
An immanent deduction (that is not idealist but rather
is based on its materiality) above all does not imply
that Man-in-person is absolutely a criminal being – an
absurd thesis, which destroys all right to defense – but
that Man-in-person is one, as we say, "radically." We
deduce the generic radicality of crime rather than its
philosophical absoluteness, which would end up justifying it. This justifies the non-sufficient necessity for
humans to be victims, and by this very fact reserves
the equally non-sufficient necessity of their prior-to-
the-first defense. As a result, the problem of a principle
of sufficient reason of crime is settled by the unilateral
complementarity that excludes both the classical and
contemporary antinomies and aporias of philosophy.

Victimological aporias

Why do we kill? But especially, and which is doubt-less worse, why do we persecute? This is the question of questions, the one before which philosophy recoils, hiding itself in the quartet of metaphysical causes: facts and history, destiny, war, and the maliciousness of men in general. Is there a principle for killing or persecuting that would not be simply a principle of absolute unrea-son, that is, still of reason? The answer to this question, if it is possible, is decisive for determining what intel-lectuals can and must do to legitimate and limit their undertaking.

Unilateral duality allows us to resolve the aporias of victimary discourse in its three forms through the marginalization of their subject, the "old man" or man in-the-world:

1. Death and continued victimization concern the sub-ject in-the-world or under philosophical obedience, and not Man-in-person. The contradiction wanted all humans, reduced to the state of individual sub-jects, to be victims of evil or sin or for none of them to be; or more generally, for all to be either once and for all mortal, or, as the religions promise us, for potentially none to be mortal.

2. The meaning of double victimization changes: it is no longer a process of division and redoubling of bodies or souls, assumed to define man from time immemo-rial. This old man is an objective appearance taken for the in-itself, but which is marginalized under the generic condition within history alone. The victim understood in-the-world would be multiple and

would result from a "separation," in reality from a division legitimately repeated such that it would be possible to say "I am already dead, or half dead." Human death is unique and results instead from a being-separated-without-separation or a being-foreclosed, not a division. The subject can die in multiple ways, but it dies once each time as a human or a Lived Experience in-the-last-instance.

3. Thus, it is possible to escape from the specular cycle of vengeance proper to the victim-become-persecutor. The no less indefinite division of victim and its persecutor, the circle of vengeance of the persecutorial victim (the victim and persecutor exchanging their roles – these are the same in the short, the long, or even the infinite term) is suppressed in the human-in-person, or at least unilateralized and confined to History. It is understood that in History left to its sufficiency, things happen circularly like this, with few exceptions. This circle is philosophy itself, deployed completely without auto-dissimulation, the form of the world and of History, that with which we make by right a history-world. The problem is to free ourselves from this bronze chain and to subject history to a practice of liberation.

4. If "resurrection" means "relief" [*relève*] or "awakening" [*réveil*], one better understands the term "reprise" – rather than repetition – which we use for the operation of the superposition of lived experiences. Reprise has the generic nature of the human subject as its condition, and complementarily, a historical occasion. There is an obligation or ultimatum to have to awaken those whom we know to be dead only to the world and to history – victims.

Let us recall the theory of the survivor. It is striking that philosophical theories do not recognize a properly and exclusively human identity for the victim, a consistency independent of the communal memory of the City, nor generally an identity that would not already be a unity and that could apply to either the Other or the Stranger without diminution or exclusion. The philosophical destiny of the victim is worse than that of nothingness, of the negative, or of "real" opposition, which at least have a history. The victim remains what it is – a waste of thought. Deconstruction gives a Greco-Judaic interpretation of these phenomena. Derrida, for example, says that narcissism pursues us to death. Obviously, he is thinking of man as a survivor damaged by death, but in no way of Man-in-person, incorruptible, whose identity – which is neither biological nor civil – cannot be reached by death, but is necessary as a negative and non-sufficient condition for thinking death. For good reason, one will say that it is impossible for man to still "exist" in his death or beyond, except that Man-in-person insists without existing, and traverses its death of an individual subject. One of the foundations of philosophy or religions is that man exhausts himself once and for all in the subject, in an anthropos endowed with language, reason, or a soul, in a being of the world, which maintains relations of co-belonging with the world and which cannot but be divided, shared, or split by death. But if death is in this way a form of divisibility, then, as was said, a second operation is legitimately necessary in this context: *dying is a continuous act and thus must take the form of victimization.* This is how thought and justice indefinitely pursue the victim by asking if they are not pursuing mankind in the individual, in short, if there is nothing but geno-cides.

From the animal persecutable in-the-last-instance to man

We have supposed that persecution is fundamental to rendering intelligible the process that allows humans to pass from the state of the animal in-the-world to the state of the In-person. No longer is anything about Man-in-person given as fact, essence, or nature by the positive sciences, which have in fact dissolved its original forms and anthropological figures, and seemed to have persecuted it in some way. As for man as not absolutely without figure but as a uniface of the Stranger – he is again before us – this will be the product of a process of generic knowledge exerted upon the material of the positive sciences. The possible generic humanization must be "desired," if not "decided," and pertains to the system of axioms expressing Man-in-person (oraxioms) destined to assure its a priori safeguarding, that is, its coming or insurrection in the world. The experience of reference of these axioms and of their formalization is this positive science that establishes the reduction of humans as animals. But this science must now become generic or futural in order for them to be defined in a new way through that "vectorial" coming. Animal object of knowledge, man is nevertheless a priori persecutable. It is as victim that he becomes human and resistant to positive persecution. He is thus not victim only as an object of occasional persecution, but more fundamentally as prior-to-the-first in-Person. The animal given or the set of sciences that represents it is only the beginning of the process or the occasion of humanization. Rather than as rational animal, we formulate Man = X by an *axiom, thus empty of positive determinations, because in-the-last-instance persecutable and thus rendered human.* The most extended persecution is aimed at the simple animal as much as at man insofar as he is also animal in general, but the ultimate cause of persecution is still elsewhere. One will remember that persecution transcends simple biological destruction only by being taken up again by philosophy, which must be debased by the resistance fighter or the Stranger we *must* become. Furthermore, the products of these conjugated variables are indeed indexed to the fully immanent factor of Man-in-person as to a complex or imaginary entity that transforms this physical or animal being into a vector, an immanental phenomenon capable of traversing history. It is not a question of a subject and a rational predicate redoubling each other in a doublet – that is rather the material of the human coming. The consequence is that if one defines man as a persecutable animal, that is, also as an animal that comes-under as vectorial, some sort of humanity by default must be accorded to it under condition, together with a certain process of transformation.

From man to "simple" animal

So what relationship is there between the "simple" animal of which humans partake and Man-in-person, which presupposes a prior-to-the-first-being of humanity and futurality?

Man holds the title of being-persecuted or victim, while the animal is persecutable only through the intermediary of man, who is himself persecuted. But if this is an original feature of man, it is certainly not a priority. Only the criminal transforms this condition of non-acting into a priority over others and over animals. The primacy of the victim does not come from the fact that it alone would know itself a victim through a supplementary reflection, but from the fact that only it has the possibility of weak resistance or transformative uprising, which the animal does not have. Man is no more victim than the animal, but as Man he is also something else through which he can experience himself as an insurrectional victim. There is no human exception from the perspective of the Good; the whole world is victimizable, and man is only exempted from the common fate through a different constitution of vectoriality and genericity. For this reason, the animal or the simple animal can be protected, that is, defended, but it cannot be treated better than man, even if sometimes it seems that way. Man-in-person is not exactly ambiguous, it is a unilateral complementarity – it is at once generic human and simple animal. It is contingently killable as a simple animal but additionally persecutable as Man-in-person, which allows it to undergo but also to defy that persecution. The animal takes on the vital inter-species or inter-individual struggle; man transposes that struggle into war and, beyond war, into generic rather than universal persecution, something the simple animal cannot do. The simple animal in humans could not rise up, start something like revolution, or resist its slaughter.

Furthermore, we have acquired a generic or non-philosophical criterion of distinction and similitude between man and animal, or more generally, between humans and the "rest" of "creation." But as there is no creation, neither is Man-in-person a kingdom in that kingdom; Man-in-Person has no priority over the animal, just a prior-priority as the power of under-determination of those beings that live as biological totality, genus, and species. There is a unilateral complementarity to be established between Man-in-person and the animal, as if the animal was a figure of the Stranger among us, such that it is the responsibility of humans that the animal itself attains, as it were through this mediation or safeguarding, the status, if one can say so, of *Animal-in-person*. By an aforementioned extension, the animal cannot be more defended than Man-in-person, but ought to be at least as much as, or along the same model as, the subject-Stranger. Human primacy is a primacy prior-to-the-first. There is no philosophical priority here, it is rather a primacy of responsibility towards every animal, and of defending humans in the very act by which they not only subjugate animals, but also assign them their last usage, an of-the-last-instance usage in which animals escape the vicious circle of slaughter, and in particular of suffering, to also become victims-in-person. The animal's fate cannot be better than that of humans, its suffering less strong than ours. Man-in-person represents the quantum of action of defense against victimization and suffering that the animal cannot hope to surpass. In this way, the occasional need to kill and consume certain animals, and in the end to exploit a large part of the earth, must also be made the object of a non-sufficient immanental deduction, or a deduction under occasion. Can we do better than a lesser evil, once it is admitted that universal and sufficient Good is a religious fantasy?

5

Insurrection and Resurrection

Victims as non-standard event

Philosophies of the event fall quickly into an antinomy linked to the most simplistic determinism and to the dialectical spirit. When the flash of its appearance has passed, either the event is only identified by its consequences, which give it substance, without being known through itself, or it is a decision that cuts across History in the greatest ignorance of the consequences. In these two forms and their averaged-out combinations, Resurrection cannot be such an event except in its post-evental "declaration" or "preaching." The unbridled voluntarism of eventality founded on forgetting and the tabula rasa of conditions is no better than the most closed off empiricism. Moreover, it is simply one, which either relies on the subject's capacity to wager (as if the wager itself didn't have some non-empirical condition and several occasions from which it is in a way inseparable) or on the negative cut with an ontological foundation (for example, mathematical or set-theoretical). Philosophy does not do justice to the complexity of the event for two unexpected reasons, which are doubtless one and the same. On the one hand, it does not know how to theorize the flash [*l'éclair*], the photo-flash [*le flash*] in the event, having at its disposition nothing but the means of phenomenological and macroscopic description without the scientific means, quantum means in particular, necessary for unfolding a flash of light. Its mathematical comprehension, as an "ungrounded" self-belonging set, is completely negative. A physical interpretation is necessary to perceive a flux of phases in the event and to seize an interlinked system of phenomena of inseparable phases in the flash of Logos, which is supposed to illuminate the cosmos and pursue its extinction in modern Reason. On the other hand, philosophy is actually the very epitome of the event. There are no events par excellence that are not philosophical; philosophy is that which makes the event by belonging to itself, by cutting itself off from every extrinsic foundation. Nevertheless, philosophy does not know itself, or forgets itself in the objects or fields characteristic to itself, in the succession of consequences and local decisions. "Know thyself": this imperative should have been aimed in-prior-priority at philosophy, which does not know itself "in-person," apprehending itself only "in-the-world" and not generically.

We reach a "quantum-inclined" theory of the event by passing onto the generic terrain. In one way or another, there is no event but the human event, and this under two complementary aspects. First, by its condition of-the-last-instance, namely a subject composed of a lived experience that is at least neutralized and capable of holding for each human – thus, generic – and of an algebraic or imaginary transcendence, simple or "short-ened" in any case, which is not necessarily the most excessive and highest, the way philosophy imagines it. Next, but complementarily, by its contingent occasion coming from the world, History, and nature, all places where determinism and realism hide, and which must be treated as symptoms. Christ, who could serve us as a model for thinking the victim as an event, meets for example the Greek and Judaic conditions, which are only occasions for his cloning from the Jewish messiahs. Christ can always be explained by this double history, but reduced to crude historical conditions there would never have been a Resurrection or a Good News, and the name of Christ would not have that real or more-than-symbolic insurrectional charge. It is necessary to exceed the duality of signifier and signified, and even the plane of the symbolic and the mathematical, to think this plane as the real itself as it rises up from (subsequent to, outside of) the reality of the world and begins in this "vectorial" and "imaginary" way its emergence as a transhistorical phenomenon. A material formalism modeled on quantum theory, and not a philosophical materialism, is the most adequate way to think the event. Christ and his resurrection, this is less a miraculous event than a non-standard or non-theological one. We would readily say, if the risk of misinterpretation were not so great, a non-event in the sense in which we normally understand the "non" opposable to philosophical sufficiency.

Insurrection, prior-to-the-first condition of resurrection

Christianity certainly has plenty of revolutionary characteristics, but usually theology crushes them in psychology and history, reducing them to belief and not faith or science as it is compacted in faith. Theology goes no further than culturally hearkening back to this revolutionary character, instead of seizing the point of radical "emergence" by which Resurrection – even more so than Revolution – is inclined to the essentially generic state of humans. To creation *ex nihilo*, to its materialist and idealist avatars, to God and the Philosopher, who both draw their decisions out of nothingness, Humans-in-person oppose a prior-to-the-first insurrection, which is revealed in the nonviolent uprising of victims. The grave is capable of this "creation"; its "void" bears no comparison to the ontological void of nothingness, just as the immanence of the One-in-One is incommensurable with the macroscopic body of Being.

Like every Christian notion forever wrongly formalized on the basis of common sense, resurrection has a negative aspect – the interruption of the cycle of natural fertility, deterioration, and rebirth – and a positive aspect, which explains this interruption – a divine eschatological gift of life that interrupts death and sin. In its turn and from a quite different point of view, this conception can be formalized anew in the quantum-oriented and generic matrix. Treated as a symptom and historico-religious model of a real and no longer phantasmatic resurrection, it undergoes the interruption of the circle of returns (as well as Christ's second coming) by the radically human or futural *eschaton* of a gift that is no longer part of life prevailing over death but of the glorious lived experience prevailing over life-death. Neither a natural phenomenon nor a religious miracle, resurrection as a generic concept is material rather than *materielle*, vectorial rather than spiritual. At each revival or superposition, it is the insurrection once each time of the immanent lived experience, traversing and debasing the most excessive monotheistic transcendences. The immediate and macroscopic notions of "death" and "life," in which Christianity tries to make heard a radicality that still escapes it, receive their full use with Man-in-person. In its radical sense, death is also "immanentized" as human, under-determined or consummated.

The generic body gets that which is glorious – and which distinguishes it from the survivor, hero, and saint – from its incorruptible or indestructible nature, from its lived-experience-without-life, not static but capable once each time of being reactivated or revived by a perpetual insurrection. This insurrection awakens it and snatches it from the pagan transcendence of the hero and the Judaic transcendence of the saint alike. It does not have the same type of separation from the rest of humans as the one carried out by transcendence, and still a different separation from the non-human remainder of creation. It is imperative that victims can make their voice heard over the whole Earth, across the abyss of death, and "call out an appeal." "Men will remember us." This is the imperative of compassion, not a call for pity. It must come from the genericity of the lived experience and its actions, rather than from the universality of "life" and the responsibility of memory dwelling in it.

A thought of victims and their defense, insofar as it for the most part comes from their prior-priority, entails a different logic of the order of time, of the generic subject as cause, and of its effect. In the Christian tradition, the glorious body is attributed to the one who is arisen; resurrection is an event that fills up the substance of the subject. But in a generic rather than a philosophical non-Christian theology, the Arisen-in-person has prior-to-the-first primacy over the operation of "resurrection," passed through or traversed by a generic immanence made up of vectors in a state of superposition. A para-doxical formula because it seems to invert the arrow of History, but no more than the notion of a priori or futural defense of victims, or more generally than the real as prior-to-the-first, which is not included in the determinist order of cause and effect forming reality. All radical immanence, "revived" by superposition or addition, carries out this same uni-version (unilateralizing inversion), which is necessary for destroying determinism when it is a question of the defense of humans. As an operation under condition of the already-Arisen, Resurrection indeed remains first, but a non-standard understanding of the Gospel implies distinguishing that which is prior-to-the-first and that which is first, which itself is placed under condition (and is thus, in short, "second"). The Arisen is in no way a survivor, which would imply an originary continuity of sublation with earthly life across death, as one could believe from the historical narrative of the Gospels and the dialectical interpretation given to them by Saint Paul, transforming the real order understood as worldly or transcendent order into a miracle destined to feed the belief of the faithful. The phenomenon of the Resurrection ought to be understood as applying especially to man and as above all not being a second creation *ex nihilo*. It is not a repetition of this miracle. In its phenomenal content, it is grasped as insurrection proper to the generic lived experience, liable to superposition and perhaps to the superposition of the two rivers, of life and of death.

***

The insurrection of victims

Let us once again confront the laughter of the cunning. Will victims have the right to "resurrection"? Because it has neither mortality nor immortality among its conditions – these are its occasions – resurrection is a specifically generic or human operation. Let us reassure the believers of little faith: to arise is not to be reborn or "to bring back to life," but to come-under as generic lived experience, to bring victims as the Future-in-person or the Insurrection that is no longer immortality. It is to affirm the primacy of the glorious body over the duplicity of the world. The Arisen come-under in the form of an ultimatum or a "last thing," an unparalleled emergence of the glorious lived experience ahead of life-death. The resurrection, understood in this insurrectional sense, is no more miraculous than survival, which is necessarily the beneficiary of an even more improbable miracle because it is the miracle such as a self-miraculating History would bestow.

The role of the future intellectual is only to help victims arise in-Man rather than mummifying them in the decidedly too inglorious shadow of memory. And here to arise is not exactly a resumption without modification of the Christian solution, which leads the dead into life or a blessed life, and which does not really succeed in escaping the pagan and natural cycle of the rebirth of the species. Taken up by philosophy, the believer always risks being a "believing animal" or a "Christian."

The Victim-in-person is the twentieth century's trademark, the symbol that records it as symptom and material. But the Victim-in-person also breaks with its sufficiency, even the one concealed by the affirmation of its finitude, as well as with the reappearances of self-proclaimed heroism. Placing History under the sign of victims or the defeated could give rise to a dolorism and a supplementary nihilism of surviving, becoming a new object of mockery; it is instead an ultimatum, a way of naming, and not just of naming but also of treating Man-in-person as the "savior" that comes-under-to-victims. Victims are the *ultimata* or the *eschata* from which we are able less to judge the world than to transform it, which has only a generic sense. It is less a question of "surpassing" the antinomy of the finitude of human life and immortal and superhuman life than of reducing it to its strictly immanent conditions and modeling it on the field of Man-in-person by showing that in the two opposing cases man is overwhelmed by a foreign and overly weighty transcendence, a doublet that is either theological and reflexive for the finite subject, or specular and infinite for the contemporary subject of the Idea. Finitary and victimary philosophies of the last century had a memory overly burdened with mortality. Some contemporary infinitarian and anti-victimarian philosophies believe themselves capable of unloading their memory with a tabula rasa, with the practice of forgetting or even of revisionism, as if it were a sign of strength and immortality. For generic humans, a single and simple transcending or ascending, rather than its doublet, suffices. They dismiss adversaries, not "back to back," but rather in the same direction, which is called "the world." The Last Instance was never anything but one single real, the Arisen-in-person. In this way, by this paradigm transformed from its Christian origin, we attempt to make ourselves a path between the Mortals of finitude and the Immortals of infinity. Oraxioms or formulas that express the Victim-in-person deal with its attributes drawn from victimology so that they are no longer attributable to Man, so that they are dis-attributed and floating in a new sphere of philo-fiction. Man-in-person makes possible a radically fictional discourse about victims – fictional insofar as the victims are never its simple objects or subjects, but its conditions and occasions.

The body of the event as clone

While awaiting broader explanations of this precession of insurrection around resurrection and of its exclusively generic meaning, we will posit that the Resurrection and the Ascension, or rather that the Arisen, its insurrection out of the grave, and its ascension, cannot follow the Crucifixion the way one common historical phenomenon follows another, but are obviously the prior-to-the-first condition that determines *a new, that is, faithful, knowledge of the Cross*. In the best of cases, Christians regard Christ as a *supra*-historical event in the history of the world, whereas he is the immanent insurrection of every resurrection. A paradigmatic event, like the sudden appearance of the flash, does not begin with an uprising of a historical or completed sort, or even with an "archi"-initial uprising. In this sense, the reified categories of the Event and the Decision remain ontological and are subverted by the oraxioms attached to the name of Christ. They must either become generic prior-to-the-first names in their turn, or remain simple materials for a knowledge that is the revived form of the Good News.

The a priori of the lived-experience-without-life,

which renders the real human, makes possible its immanent extension to the problem of the victims and functions as their a priori defense. Christ is less the example or figure of this ultimatum than its oraxiomatic name. Even Christ, to say it in Greek, is the paradigm of the victim, but this primacy of exception is meaningless outside of Man-in-person, of Christ understood as the last real still to come to counter-history. Crucifixion by the world, philosophy, and religion together: this is the status of every victim, the subject in its individual transcendence as a direct object of persecution. But only a subject that brings resurrection with it, not an object subjected to an operative passivity, can "arise." A thoroughgoing glorious materiality, not the ideality of the hero, is separated from every eternity of the world, for which it is nevertheless a priori destined in order to consummate its knowledge and transform it. The world as persecutor of Christ must also be given "in-person" for Christ to be Persecuted and Savior at the same time and for his response to God's abandonment to be complete.

The oraxiomatic name of Christ is performative in a special way: it is a real rather than a logical decision, an oraxiom that grounds the faith of the faithful. How can we understand that a saying is real "at the same time" and that it is "itself" its determining condition? Only in-the-last-instance and as an under-determined declaration in a unilateral complementarity. An oraxiom is not an irrational miracle, the realization or the possibility of an impossible. Saying as confession is an oraxiom when saying-the-Resurrection or declaring-Christ – without being thoroughly a transcendent sacramental symbol or a profession of subjective faith or, still worse, a belief – is immediately unilateralized and lived as a phenomenon of cloning. The name of Christ is not strictly identical to Christ himself or is only so in-the-last-instance and arouses the real of faith or the kerygma as clone. When I say the Resurrection, I am the clone of the Arisen, but we must not be content to "say" it. It is a quantum-oriented practice, that is – to recapture the mystical ways – an undulatory breathing and a superpositional and particulate outburst ("God is dead! Christ has arisen!")

6
Our Ordinary Messiahs

Puppets of the powers or clones of the victims?

We will not ask the future-oriented intellectual to flee real history, the politics of the day, or the evolution of mores, but to stop adhering to them in the name of the trinity duty-memory-responsibility and the very equivocal modern refusal of the "beautiful soul." Too often, he thinks to warn future victims in the name of past victims because, even when he intends to struggle against genocides, he does so for reasons that exceed him and transcend the spectacle of crimes that make up the matter of History. On a theoretical level, his practice duplicates History: it is a miniaturization of facts to the dimensions of bad conscience, prolonging victimization without really explaining anything. Here, we object to him for lacking the theoretical means, not for analysis or ideas – often he has too many of those – but for "dualysis" of conjunctures, and for fighting in the name of local, partisan, and communitarian ideals, and more generally for fighting under the banner of victims, putting himself on the side of force without knowing it. This is the contradiction of the dominant intellectual: he produces in theory a redoubling of the empirical mess that guides his actions and explains his mediatic sufficiency. Every intellectual born directly or, even worse, indirectly of philosophy is a "totalitarian" feigning ignorance of this fact. To "imitate" victims does not imply an identification, a specular and contemplative imitation, or a way of beating one's breast. Against the puppets of power we put forward clones – yes! – the clones of victims that intellectuals could be. The dominant intellectual interpellates victims, even "inspects" them; the generic intellectual imitates them the way a clone to a certain extent imitates its original material.

The Victim-in-person, of which human essence is the superposition, is not Man's constituent predicate, whether analytic or synthetic. From this point of view, it is not possible to determine the Victim-in-person by means of objective relations alone. The more doctors, lawyers, and intellectuals there are to look after it in a sufficient and authoritarian way, the more its generic essence is likely to remain indeterminate. On the other hand, one can transform the intellectual so that he, as future intellectual, takes up the Victim-in-person's set of relations. But, someone will object, if we can no longer directly help the victim the way we remedy the flaws of an object or an idea, what's the point? What good is the work of that intellectual who seems to be a carrier of fictions [*porte-fiction*], declaring overly utopian messages too boldly? He precisely does not declare the victim the way one declares a historic event or the way the imagination invents a religious utopia. He declares what happens, and happens perpetually in the very quasi-performative act of the declaration, like one who transforms society and history according to the victims that never cease to arrive. Instead of reaching the victim through a horizon of preliminary being, of having a pre-comprehension of the victim as of a universal, he superposes himself on the victim *in a practical way, assuming it "in-person" or taking care of it without distance or relation.* The act of the intellectual, determined in-the-last-instance in this way, is a transformation of the discourse of history and society, of philosophy and the religions, but it transforms them without addressing them ecstatically, without being devoted to them as objects or destined for them as ends.

The intellectual under condition, neither subject nor object but vector of action

A double constraint – not contradictory because immanent in-the-last-instance and allowing action – is exerted on and under-determines the intellectual in-the-world. The first constraint, both globally necessary and locally contingent, is that of events with their historical background. The intellectual cannot but be guided by that which is presented through the media as the victim, but this is no more than a simple indication or occasional cause for the generic intellectual. The second constraint, which is really prior-to-the-first, is that every victim is a victim under the *materielle* and a priori (material) condition of being a Human-in-person. Acting *for* the singularity of the occasion that motivates him, or on it as on a material, the intellectual must conceive of an intervention beyond that singularity. He does not settle for taking a stand, but allows himself to be under-determined by a generic universality that applies, undivided, to classes, nations, and cultural and ethnic differences. His action is motivated or initiated by a muddled local conjuncture made of superposed decisions, but it has a univocal intention for every victim once each time. "All men" or humanity – this can still be *a parti pris*, a way of dividing and setting humans against each other (the all is only philosophically accessible as divided or locally limited); it repeats persecution a second time. Intellectual acting must be indivisible for each subject-Man as ultimately generic. An indivisible action in fact presupposes that *Man-in-person is never what philosophy calls the object or subject of action*, that it does not decide who is or is not a human victim according to an empirical, biological, transcendental, or religious evaluative scale which would be imposed upon the victim by a transcendent objectivity. The being-victim is of no use for measuring or classifying humans; *it renders them non-separable without dividing them in order to reach them again.* As Man-in-person, the victim is an absent or vanished referent; it is unrepresentable, and only representable (but it is already too late) precisely when it is in the grip of a process of victimization. As for the rest, that is, for the most part – it is thinkable vectorially.

One suspects that, if there must be some sort of "intellectual" action, political or otherwise, it will result from a certain neither clearly analytical nor explicitly synthetic complementarity of the victim to be defended and the intellectual who possesses the means of acting. He must act according to the Victim-in-person, or take care of its non-acting within his own proper means, its silence within his speech. But why and how can this unification be made, which is not ordered as self-defense or legally normalized, and is prescribed by the victim alone by means and with the means of the intellectual. The generic intellectual is authorized by the Victim-in-person alone and not his own self, accepting its defense a priori. Between the two of them there is what we call a non-relation, which is strong analytically and weak synthetically, and which we have explained elsewhere. This is the only way to wrest victims from the bad conscience of intellectuals, from memory's repeated iterations as duty or work, and to consider them as our *ordinary messiahs*. If there are victims, and they are there as soon as we, well-meaning, treat man as a rational animal, we must and can treat them in a manner called human in-the-last-instance only by making use of the immanent matrix of Man-in-person, like an ultimatum that comes-under to the sufficiency and transcendent finalities of the intellectual and "his" victim. In Man-in-person's practice, there seemingly is something like a ground of quietism, but its true force is not the self-negation of its acting but the calm non-acting, which is acting or resisting even the world as its correlate, rather than acting on its particular objects. Have we not reproached the West and its philosophy enough for not being able to act upon the particular, for aiming too far away (and being too revolutionary) or else for aiming too close by? The specific acting of human non-acting does not seek to reach the faraway and total world, nor the empiria that occupies it, but to reach *once each time* the world as *ultimate* form of the singular and the particular.

A victim-oriented matrix and its axiom-subjects

The philosophical self-destruction of humanism is one thing, but the destruction of the empirical figure of man by the human, social, and cultural sciences is another one altogether. Yet they hold hands at the two ends of the chain such that the intellectual sees his object vanish or crumble and scatter. From now on, the new problem for the philosopher is to still be able to act, but this time for Man and according to Man and, despite the absence or disappearance of the human object, to institute a Man-without-humanism and thereby the most adequate concern for the victim. The last intellectual act still possible, not positively scientific, we have said, is to claim Man as a simple symbol or first term of an axiom, indeed the prior-to-the-first term of an oraxiom, but without object and thought becoming reciprocally identified with each other in the classically philosophical way. A special axiom, which we have called "oraxiom," determined in-the-last-instance by Man-in-person, a unilateral complementarity, on the one hand, of its "object," for which it prescribes the treatment, and on the other, of its "subject" as ultimate condition of this prescription. This condition allows one to use again, one last time, for example, Christian humanism, and not just the anthropological disciplines, which are not always empty of philosophical sufficiency, but which can nevertheless be transformed into forces of production for a new ethics. "Man" is thus a simple vector, even a posed-without-position, truly the Real in its immanence of "superposition," under-determining condition of every ethical position, and the only possible "reflexivity" of the oraxiom.

The oraxiom is a way of using the silence of humanist discourse and even the sufficient practice of the persecutor. It is the generic intellectual way of "imitating" the victim by resisting the persecutor or de-potentializing his weapons. Several features characterize the oraxiom in contrast to the classic axiom:

1. Far from being logico-formal and marking ethics with a logical formalism – Kantian, for example – it is algebraically formal but lived, objectively idempotent but material (material formalism), prepared as a superposition of utterances, which serve as its variables. It is a vector of thought.
2. It is devoid of the sufficiency of reality, but not devoid of all reality, because it arranges as clones the contents of philosophical ethics and the human sciences, which are simple variables or forces of production.
3. These forces of the oraxiom are simply transformative and productive of new "finalities" as properties of Man-in-person; they are themselves under-determined, globally simplified or debased in comparison to the old ethical finalities proposed by philosophy and its humanism.
4. They cannot themselves be of use to the work of under-determination except within a special arrangement, within an intellectual matrix that conjugates philosophy and a physical science – quantum science – destined to replace logic and Kantian formalism, for example, or phenomenology as science in the most contemporary ethics. There is no ethics without explicit or implicit (Heidegger, by his refusal of science in the definition of *Dasein*) recourse to a science.

5. This matrix is victim-oriented or victim-inclined because it conjugates the persecutor and the persecuted by being under-determined by the victim rather than by the persecutor.

6. It produces ethical effects because they belong to the prior-to-the-first defense of humans against the thought-world, its doublets, and its double transcendence.

7. Lastly, these ethical effects are concretely interpretable by the sciences and humanism, which are their transcendent models responding to the conditions of the world. If one gives up the vicious circles of the thought-world, then the only solution is to use this matrix to de-Christianize Christian notions, de-Judaize Jewish notions, de-Islamicize Islamic notions, and place them all in the service of the defense of those who have been their victims. It is not a question of carrying out a negation of these cultures but of ensuring their mutation into materials and thus also into models of the new ethics.

The imitation or cloning of the victim by the intellectual

It will have been necessary to abandon philosophical authority and make a leap into Man-in-person in order to adopt the victim and act according to it in-person. A non-vicious action of the intellectual that does not multiply the victim is only possible if Man, who is in the victim and "represented" by it, clones a subject or an agent-victim, the intellectual, from the historical victim. We have called generic or under-determined intellectual the one who intervenes under the condition of the Victim-in-person. Doubtless, he chooses his victims from among those imposed upon him, but it is not they who make him act against philosophy in this way. It is a question of renewing through cloning under the last-instance the classic thematic of the Imitation of Christ as the In-person having itself ceased to be the Greco-Christian imitation of God. In this sense, the imitation of the Victim-in-person can be the watchword for the action of generic intellectuals, who use a process of cloning that is obviously not biological because it brings into play the glorious or immanent body.

The victim is a victim of the world or of a force that passes through the attraction of the world. But through a point in itself, which is its a priori human nature, it does not participate in the world or is separated from it; this is their unilateral complementarity. If we fail to acknowledge such a being-separated or foreclosed of Man, we would be enchanted by an antinomy, completely engaged in a process of interminable and permanent victimization without hope of salvation, or protected once and for all against all persecution. The action of the intellectual would either be hopeless and even impossible, or would victimize a bit more. We laid down as an axiom that Man-in-person is not absolutely or definitively a victim, that it is a victim "radically," that the victim by its essence is defended a priori, not only because it can be persecutorial in its turn (that does not resolve the problem) but because it is the condition for taking the victim seriously or granting it the real. It is a question of not drowning men in a blurred claim of victimization, but of retaining a certain delimitation of the victim status, even if the victim is there in "every" man and not merely in a select few.

"Victim-in-person" is an expression that could stave off philosophical haste. The intellectual cannot base himself on the represented victim, whether local or general ("all"), which is only the occasional cause of his activity; he must by contrast identify with the Victim-in-person as with his non-representable cause. Not missing or absent, as psychoanalysts or certain philosophers say about the cause or the real, but positively invisible except as unifacial or Strange. There is a positivity of the invisible or the indiscernible as the negative or non-sufficient condition of the manifestation of the thought-world. This insistence of the non-visible passes from Man to the world *via* the subject that it clones precisely from the world, like a transfer of in-person human identity to the world. However, a simple identification of the intellectual with Man as negative cause risks repeating the philosophical hallucination of a transcendent and graspable identity. It is thus less an identification than an assumption of the Real in the form of a practice of superposition of the lived experiences that constitute the In-person.

Of course, the only proof of this intellectual assumption of Man is the new practice of the means of speech and writing. It is determined by the silence of-the-last-instance, which is that of Man in the victim. A use of speech or the form-world, it does not prohibit speaking – to the contrary – but it under-determines the sufficiency of its speech by its weakness in-the-last-instance. The subject as victim lets out crying words, which are axioms denuded of philosophical meaning. Even when it is a "no!," this radical no is addressed to the sufficiency of the world without possible appeal. The intellectual conveys this vanished speech, forcing it beyond all vanishing, even into the logic of the world that it affects. This is the de-philosophication of Logos, the de-Christianization of the Word, the de-Judaization of the Torah, something else entirely than deconstruction or de-mythization; it is their human or weak oraxiomatization, our imitation of Christ.

If the subject-victim is forced to be silent and thus comes close to coinciding with its being-human, silent by definition, does this not risk justifying torture once again, whatever one might say? Torture is the reduction of the Man-in-person to the subject, and every reduction of this sort is a return to a being of man as *torsion*. The *torturer* [*tortionnaire*] lives on this dangerous ambiguity; the persecutor glorifies the subject, as does philosophy, which exercises a theoretical torsion, something that should be revisited. The cries of torture are either the axioms by which the victim resists or exercises its ultimate humanity, or philosophically the simulations or the appearances of an axiom, the cries of the rational animal, that is, the philosophies. This is an uncertainty about "man" left in the hands of the world, in a hand-to-hand fight with the unforeseeable outcome. Instead of hiding in ethnic, political, moral, and cultural generalities, which destroy the human intelligibility and generic universality of phenomena, let us pose the problem of intellectual assistance for victims on other grounds, for example ethical but not moral, non-philosophical rather than ontological. Instead of posing the problem in plurivocal terms, let us give a univocal "definition" of Man for all subjects grappling with history. An ethics will pose Man as philosophically indefinable but oraxiomatically treatable. Even if Man in his solitude and non-sufficiency cannot struggle against this general harassment, if he needs the subject and its operation because persecution in any case implies them, it is in Man-in-person that the radical cause of victimization is in the same gesture concealed and denounced.

The future-oriented intellectual

As for what we have called the futurality of the Arisen, the Victim-in-person is the prior-to-the-first symbol according to which it becomes possible to think history, even the history of the Resurrection; it is the cornerstone of the science of humanity on the ruins of the human sciences. The victim has always been understood in a historicizing and backwards-looking way as a phenomenon that draws its being-real from memory, as a function of the past, of destiny, of war, of the gravitational forces of society. It is surreptitiously or explicitly discarded in the losses and gains of a history constructed out of suffering, out of cruelty and stupidity, out of death and memory. This is a way of finding it a principle of reason after the fact. But, furthermore, the crime, and even persecution (an abstraction made of *ex post facto* explanations), is so incomprehensible, absurd, and deprived of sense that this absence of reason, this excess of pure presence or actual transcendence, presents in relief the possible affect of a new future, apparently "opposed" to this representation, which pretends to *suffice* for "thinking" victims.

Crime is somewhat similar to an accident in a technological circuit; it makes the victim shine at least for a brief moment before throwing it back into a form of vanishing, either in memorial survival, the flat light of screens and the demi-logos of the media, or in the radical immanence of the generic lived experience. Nevertheless, the crime, unlike the accident, has a human correlate directly and not secondarily. Nothing here has the inert status of a tool (apart from its being taken in hand, which even then is not the same type of immanence). Crime is already an attempt to transcend a history once and for all, among other things a history of the "mean" or the "tool" object. But the victim is not a tool to be damaged or capital to be destroyed; its essence is generic. And instead of appearing only to disappear or to survive, like a tool in the immanent circuit of being (of ontological pre-comprehension), it disappears radically in order to, perhaps, "survive" and moreover to be "revived" by superposition in Man-in-person.

What then would it mean to "survive" in an immanent way? How would it be possible since the criminal can exceed himself in transcendence and even master himself a second time? A decisive and doubtless new nuance must be introduced between transcendence and immanence. This is an overly simple opposition: transcendence is always double transcendence, doublet of itself even though it seems simple and given all at once to philosophy. Immanence, across philosophers like Spinoza, Nietzsche, and Deleuze, is also too simple, unitary. In reality, the immanence of the Real is necessarily the vectorial ascender that begins transcending it, and whose principal property is to be superposable or addable with another ascender, that is, with itself. Put another way, it is vectorial, analytically strong and synthetically weak. The insurrectional ascender does not redouble itself in or around an object but draws its consistency from superposing itself with an other. The victim is not a flat, logical identity coinciding with itself;

it *rises up* as immanence that remains in itself. It must be admitted that there is a true uprising of victims, and that in this form they can under-determine the crime and the criminal, de-potentializing or making them "decline." This simple or unilateral uprising does not withdraw into itself and does not necessarily become revolutionary, but it must be taken up and revived by the intellectual compelled to a future-thought. If not as memory and phantoms, victims do not return a second time; they come-under from No Where and in No Time as real-virtual, and constitute the force of subversion whose other name is futurality.

The immanence of the One in relation to Being is not that of Being in relation to being. It is invisible but unforgettable. It is fit to suspend or annul all at once the grandeur of the barely committed crime; the excess of transcendence is placed under condition of radical immanence, which renders the crime measurable and subject to judgment by the victim, at least in-the-last-instance. The victim that knows itself obscurely to be a victim manifests its criminal as such, which is to say that the criminal is immediately "accused" and judged by the victim, which does not need to resort to vengeance but can control and institutionalize that vengeance through justice. Vengeance responds to conditions that are supposedly external to the process of a priori defense and asserts the in-itself autonomy of crime, whereas for its part the victim is assumed to not know it but simply undergo it. But the criminal and the crime are "interiorized" and manifested, as it were, and justice is rendered immanent "in-person" as far as possible. It is in this way that victims are the "cornerstone" of humanity, executioners included.

Why is the future in the hands of victims, which seem

instead to be the past of humanity? Because of their human essence, which makes them *ultimata*, the last, that is, prior-to-the-first, beings to "judge" the world. The judgment of the world is not "last" except in the sense of prior-to-the-first. If there were only the past, only buried bodies consumed by death, there would be no victims; human non-consistency, which resists the world not directly but indirectly, must be the essence-of-coming of victims as *ultimata* and not of beasts consuming each other. To crime and persecution, we do not contrast the memorial treasure of past victims, which would serve us as a protective wall, victims re-anticipated by a bad catastrophism, inserted into a preformatted future. Instead, to them we contrast "born-victims," which humans and sometimes humans still to be born are. They bear witness to the Future-in-person and compel us to accept, against all justification, that there have been victims at various moments and for various historical reasons. The born-victims, even those yet to come, are capable of rising up, and it is this sort of insurrection that was called "resurrection." Already, that there are victims that are not yet born remains incomprehensible, unjustifiable, and induces a different temporal affect than history and memory, the affect of the most achronic future, of the Last Instance. These victims who come to us as if to be born make the present appear as belonging already to the past and retain it suspended in its own fall, the fall of its criminal sufficiency.

On compassion as insurrection

It is a paradox that will appear easy. Really, intellectuals have always positioned themselves alongside the strong and alongside the State, when not alongside the Churches, and even alongside the victims when they believe the victims to be "strong" and capable of *absolutely reversing* a situation, to the point of becoming – in the contemporary age, following their failure – puppets of the most mediocre power. When they criticized the State or religions, nations or communities, and when they took the side of victims, it was often because victims seemed to them to be a force capable of subverting the actual or present order of the world, of dialectically rebelling against war and ignorance. How, in these conditions and with this belief, do we not return to a flat conformism? But it is a question, to take up a Kierkegaardian dialectic, *either* of denying the world, of making it march better to the crack of the whip, or of transforming it and awakening the prior-to-the-first defense of victims, their weak power of insurrection. *Or again, either* a "strong thought," always newly directed towards a hallucinated superhuman destination, threatened with downfall and ruin, or a thought of ensuring that history will not be buried even amidst the stars.

For example, in certain eras language is particularly corrupted by politicians, the military, the religious, the advertisers, the media, and the intellectuals themselves – in their indecency, each is propaganda. An irrepressible nausea seizes individuals, logically forcing them to revolt, to become poets, writers, sometimes philosophers, sometimes scientists. In various forms, the suicides of language, survivors of paleonymies, glorifiers of new idioms, we cannot always evaluate the degree of insurrectional intensity that animates them. But such an insurrection of victims that occurs in and with language should attract intellectuals. Mocked pity, overused compassion, these are also the problems of a linguistic insurrection, which is different from a "linguistic turn." The nineteenth century abused "pity" – Nietzsche and Marxism vilified this easy acquisition of good conscience. Then the media killed "compassion," divulged the "compassionate," and made State use of it. Like all linguistic and poetic revolts, would this not be precisely a task for intellectuals: to save even a word, this word, from the official disaster that has become common, to contrast a glorious use of the victim's terms to a media philosophy of intellectuals? Will we replace the victimary ideology of pity with a new "fiction," that of the Glorious Victim, undoubtedly a thought *for* victims, but which does not allow itself to be determined by their representation or by their existence, never taking them for its referent, but succeeding in detaching them from the world where they have suffered? This would be called a resurrection, compassion that brings back from the dead. Recalling the distinction between life and the lived-experience-without-life, we would rather say that victims and their words come like lived experiences from among the-living-and-the-dead, and that the insurrection of compassion is in coming-under before us. A glorious thought is an arisen thought, ordinary in a sense, carrying out not the resentment of a philosophy, but imitation by cloning the victim. Why not a philo-fiction of victims rather than their memorial survival?

What is the real condition of possibility of compassion? That extra step that we have never stopped taking: *what is the Real of or in the practical possibility* of affects for the victim? This step is decisive; one no longer asks what is the empirico-transcendental mechanism of an affect, its ideal a priori possibility; this would already be to surpass it towards an object. We ask what is the real or material (lived) mechanism of its use by Man-in-person? Moreover, the Real is never a "mechanism," but the operation of insurrection that clones a subject and transforms the affects that it related for the first time to the world. Its philosophical, ethical, and psychological explanations being of little import, what is to be done with these affects, whose most clandestine kernel is compassion, such as they exist? With the a priori of Man-in-person as glorious body, a new material – rather than materialist or spiritualist – usage of the old ethics is possible; this is our exclusively human "care" for the Victim-in-person, its philosophies, and its principles. If pity belongs to overexposed victims, care as compassion belongs, by means of "oraxioms," to the most secret of future victims not yet born. For many reasons, pity is not foreign to the piety due to the dead, even though it is not its simple doublet and enriches it with new determinations. Compassion is distinguished from pity by its content: (1) victims are the ordinary messiahs of intellectuals; they serve them – at least ordinarily – as a transcendental guide; (2) they are also, we can now add, the only messiahs that intellectuals imitate or of which they are the clones; (3) lastly, they are prompted, motivated, and helped to arise by generic intellectuals. More deeply, compassion is distinguished by its extreme weakness, the non-acting of the victim as weak force in relation to the strong forces that persecute it in the world. Nevertheless, unpower is insurrectional (this is a paradox for determinist representation, and one that must be dismantled) because non-acting is the radical non-acting of the prior-to-the-first insurrection. Like a passive insurrection, an "impossible" or causeless ascent, it is without a doubt the principle of the real as quantum and not as worldly, macroscopic, and determinist. Insurrection is the very structure of the human real, its vectoriality. Given its non-sufficient necessity, it needs only an occasion or a persecution so that, like the basso continuo of the lived experience, it persists in care. Such a weak force, above all if its origin is immanent by superposition, is certainly not an absolute absence of intervention, a shortage or lack of action. The minimal prior-to-the-first action of insurrection is necessarily passive, a power vested with a last powerlessness. We are positing that insurrection understood in this way is the essence of compassion of care.

Compassion is the specific non-acting of all acting within affect as determined in-the-last-instance by this non-acting. Its confusion with a psychological content, a "sentiment" (or even, in Schopenhauer, with a universal metaphysical content), makes it difficult to understand that the generic lived experience is its ultimate condition and above all its condition of immanence. It renders accessible to us, as interferents, other subjects as Strangers with whom we superpose ourselves as persecuted or denied. Compassion is not the doing of heroes and is not aimed at them except through derision or a superior form of love, with the result that certain traces of compassion appear even in victims with regard to their persecutors.

The dream of victims

With each new object or theme, we have covered several phases of the same curve: the intellectual doxa of victims, the conditions of a theoretical seizure of their problem, then their weak force and their resistance, the possibility of an ethics for intellectuals and philosophers, and finally their messianic character, the new function that they could assume in relation to us. It is, some would say, a very classic curve – theory, ethics, religion – the trajectory of a fully deployed humanism. Without denying this quite objective appearance, we will note that to approach here a relation to the divine is in reality to plunge into the generic human, to debase the plan of salvation to the status of a property of man, and to render this plan of salvation definitively non-calculable for God himself. Too many victims have muddled its architecture and erased a large part of its traceability. In this disaster of theology, this fall of philosophy, a single question remains (evidently out of reach of intellectuals): *who deserves to arise, who is able to? We have already answered: it is victims because they bring the most sufficient thought – that of life-death – to its knees.* Is it not the ultimate trap to once more kneel down at the foot of the Cross, of the Victim-par-excellence, to lay down the arms of Reason before Folly? What counts as non-calculable in the plan for salvation is not the Cross – too foreseeable – but the Resurrection. It is not the visible Crucified, the victim offered up to the concupiscence of believers, but the spectral Arisen of the Christophanies. Stripped of the rags of Christian belief, what remains of the Resurrection is what constitutes its prior-to-the-first condition, its radical kernel of Insurrection, the uprising by which the new realm of humans begins. If the Christ named "Jesus" was born to be crucified as an exemplary victim, he is also made to come, rather than to return, as Inrisen [*Inssuscité*]. Our last fidelity is to the Insurrection: such is the Gospel-fiction.

Towards a non-standard ethics for the use of the philosophers

Several contemporary problems:

1. First, the traditional one of the possible insertion of the term "Holocaust" into discourse. Not into history, whether the insertion is justified or not (this derivative philosophico-intellectual problem is not our object), but into philosophy (under it, on its fringes, as an exception, as the foundation, etc.). It is thus not a question of an intervention into an exchange of politico-intellectual arguments or "ideas" (of which we are incapable), or of taking or not taking sides on its philosophical meaning, and even less on its historical, political, and factual meaning, even if it is impossible not to think starting from this "event" in such a way that it can persecute us *before even "questioning" us.* The Holocaust is perhaps too excessive to be a simple event and to be left to the intellectuals, or even to the philosophers. Instead, we will suppose that Christ and the Holocaust, the Good News and the Unforgivable News, in spite of everything, are comparable as foundational or re-foundational events, despite their apparently opposed interpretation, which deserves to be deepened. If such events have nothing "natural" about them, in the sense that they exceed "nature" in all of its philosophical definitions, they also have nothing simply "historical" about them. We must be the "contemporaries" (Kierkegaard) of these events, something that is certainly not – for reasons drawn from both quantum physics and Judaism – a question

of simultaneity or co-presence. It is at least (in expectation of a more thorough interpretation of this formula, which still perhaps conceals an appearance) the non-place or the non-time where man finally reveals that he wants to and can persecute man beyond all imagination, transcendental or religious. It is a revelation that obliges this time the philosopher to jump whether he likes it or not into a responsibility that is no longer necessarily "my" responsibility, as Levinas still says. It is understood that this is a revelation of Evil beyond all nature or history. Even Christ, in revealing sin in a less mythological form, more generic than religious or "ancient," had to rebel against philosophy as the revelation of the Good. In addition, Christ and the Holocaust, all else being different, have the same sort of force (but doubtlessly a greater one) as Kant's philosopheme of "radical evil," the flip side of the rational fact of moral judgment. They are "generic" events, that is, ones capable of compelling us to humble the power of the philosophical horizon, to make knowledge "decline" as a simple means. If we admit the now-common question, how to still think after Auschwitz or "in" Auschwitz, but also how not to be forced to think, it cannot be with the secret hope of saving the certainly lessened or wounded authority of philosophy one last time, of allowing a mastery to subsist, for example a deconstructive one, which would be that of the question itself. As far as we are "contemporaries" of victims, it is as difficult for Christians to think (Greek) or not to think otherwise after Christ as for Jews after the Holocaust. Perhaps we have better things to do than to "question" ourselves again and forever. This is the meaning of the inevitable introduction of a non-Good, a "homeopathic" dose of Evil at the expense of philosophy.

2. Next, the problem of "exemplarity." It seems difficult to pose the problem of extreme persecution, like that of the Jewish people, in terms of absolute exception or of exemplarity, an infinite and finally theologico-theoretical transcendence like a Judaic Platonism. As always, this is to immediately take a historical fact, as terrifying as it is, for an absolute. Already for traditional philosophy, this is a nonsense, the refusal of all mediation. This reaction of victims, which raises persecution to the status of concept or thought, really has no *sense*, or too much sense, or sense that is too ill-situated, and amounts to the reduction of its impact. Levinas is their witness; without much modification, he transposes persecution into philosophy *and in its place* (consequently, an ethics of the passivity of the hostage without much hope for resistance). On the other hand, those who were not direct victims, but who are nonetheless "contemporaries" of these victims, will be inclined to make the following distinction: what are the theoretical effects with which the Holocaust globally affects philosophy, as opposed to what are its effects "in" philosophy? They want a certain restriction, not on the history and sociology of the Holocaust, but on its claim in Levinas's work to act as a substitute for philosophy. It is a question of bringing insurrection to philosophy, rather than substituting something for it in a more or less direct way. It is necessary to restrict the Holocaust as an absolute example in order to remake a space for the consistency and universality

of a philosophical *type*. One could use the same argument about Jonas, who limits classical theology in such a way that it is also almost a substitution. Doubtlessly, persecution traumatizes philosophy but cannot hope to act as a substitute for it; rather, it gives rise to a certain matrix-like future-inclined conjugation of the variables of Judaism and philosophy. This matrix inverts the Greek or philosophical side and its desired domination over the Judaic side, but only inverts it by superposing the two sides in the form of a new experience, of a lived experience that is neither Greek nor Jewish, that which we call a philo-fiction through vectorial insurrection.

The great Greco-Judaic disagreement [*différend*], which cut across the philosophy of the last century, is resolved in the victim as a vector that bears the human in-prior-priority of History. With the Holocaust as occasion, and additionally with Christ as condition, we have become inextricably Jews and Greeks, perhaps not in the manner of deconstruction, but we have ceased to be totally or exclusively spontaneous, or Greek, philosophers. The whole problem is to think this new "unsharing" [*impartage*]. To depart from Levinas and from infinite persecution, a form of mediation is necessary, still supposing a constitutive function of philosophy. It is accomplished in Derrida's work by the adjoining of two sufficiencies, of the sufficient Greek Logos and of the Jewish Other, also completely sufficient (this is the GreekJew and the JewGreek). It is thus a conjugation of instances, but it does not succeed quantumly because it is not made in an immediately vectorial way. We carry out this intrication through an *immediate mediation* obtained by the superposition of Logos and the One-in-One, of Being and Man-in-person, a procedure that can only take place in a quantum milieu, and not in a linguistic or a textual one. Our solution is that of the "Last Instance" as primacy of prior-to-the-first messianity over philosophy to which this messianity has direct access.

3. Finally, let us tackle "crime against humanity," a broad generic formula that is too quickly philosophized, suspected of humanism, and reduced to the juridical. First it would be necessary to elucidate the concept of humanity, at the risk of returning to a vague approximation of the "rights of man." As soon as man is named anywhere, at the fore of a watchword, he is an empty universal, a generality assailed by the usual suitors – nations, societies, or communities – with their well-known claims. We must clarify: *every crime is in the end, in-the-last-instance, a crime against humanity*, but why? The "against" is here insufficient even if it is carried out against the subject (the criminal confuses Man and the subject); it is hallucinatory in its intention or in the desire for murder, but not in its actuality, which is more complex. One can only murder in a way different from beasts among themselves when guided by a hallucination in which the worldly or historical subject *seems* to exhaust the humanity of Man. For reasons that are at root theoretical, we refuse to fall into a victimology that is a part, indeed the foundation, of victimary ideology. It is not unexpected to be anti-victimophile on a theoretical plane if it is admitted that this theoretical plane is not autonomous, that it is in-the-last-instance under human condition,

and that the practical defense of victims is a radical (rather than absolute) imperative and is so only under this condition.

Restatement of the overall argument

1 What happens in the victim/criminal couple is incomprehensible insofar as it falls back upon forms of ordinary causality, internal to the world and applying to non-human regions of reality. It is doubtless also a phenomenon of conjuncture, an occasional and represented event, but we attempt to free it, as such, from its ontological coating. The victim has an exceptional positive force of revelation; it is a real phenomenon "before" being a first concept or an abstraction, before falling under a logos. It is radically pre-predicative, or more precisely, prior-to-the-first for every first predicate, which means that every theory of the victim, and every predicate position, is under-determined as real in-the-last-instance by its "object."

2 The non-victimizable Man and the subject-victim introduce a new form of causality and a new form of exclusively unilateral relation. The victim is understood as a mode of this duality, either as an a priori-of-resistance or an a-priori-resistance to the world and its criminality. Outside of this a priori resistance, the victim is interpreted, for example, in a Judaic way as an incomprehensible absolute passivity. Once it is understood as an effect of destiny or of the history-world, or as a hostage of God, the victim is twice victim and thus defeated; this is *the passivity of the victim interpreted in a Greco-Judaic way*. By contrast, the problem of its

phenomenon is to make the victim appear once each time, and thenceforth to make possible a struggle based upon it. Its specific force comes from resistance to the force-of-force that crushes and crowns this crushing by conceptualizing it. This is a vision of Man far removed from Greek destiny or Judaic persecution, even though tragedy as well as the misfortune of the hostage perfectly illustrate the passivity of the victim incapable of showing its real phenomenon or its substance.

3 A simple affirmation or identification of the macroscopic entities of the victim and the criminal would in the end turn necessarily to the "phenomenological" advantage of the criminal. To reduce this risk without definitively suppressing it at the same time, it is necessary to treat the two parties according to the duality of a matrix. The first operation sets down a causality or a reciprocal interpretation between the victim and the criminal, which presuppose each other in obviously heterogeneous relations, but whose inverse products have not yet revealed their true relation. The true relation appears with a second operation that affects this reciprocity by accentuating either the criminal, who is repeated or redoubled as an index, or the victim, equally repeated or redoubled as an index. Let us examine the first case. This indexing to the criminal is his way of returning to the scene of the crime; it finishes transforming the reciprocity of variables into a reversibility or equality of inverted products. This primacy of the criminal, representing victorious force, has an affinity with philosophy, despite appearances. It is secretly valorized by the admiring horror and heroic memory it arouses. In other words, the duality of the criminal and the

victim is overdetermined by philosophy, which can only valorize the criminal. This is the point of view of the justice-world or history, which cannot really pursue the criminal because it can only reinforce or redouble him, manifesting him in his glory, pardoning him by effacing him in the sphere of transcendence. Generally, in this case the victim is valorized in the media for its passivity, which demands pity and a different memory (ceremonies, acts, history). Its glory and that of the criminal co-belong to each other and are distinguished, sometimes weakly, indeed being identified with each other to the point of losing their qualitative difference. This philosophical solution, dialectical or transcendental, returns to an unequal sharing out of justice; in reality, it overvalues the admired and positively celebrated criminal, while it depreciates or in the end undervalorizes the victim, which is destined for the nasty role of vengeance and "doing justice," for the pitiful glory of making demands, as the claimant of reparation and compensation.

The second indexing is to the victim. A more just justice than philosophical justice, one that allows the transformation of philosophical justice rather than a passive submission to it, and demands the accentuation of the victim's role as that which comes to affect the products of variables. It is important to accept rather than refuse the victim as this new media value that it has become but to no longer understand it completely the way philosophy or its sufficiency does, that is, through transcendence alone, through destiny or history, to not reduce it, for example, to being only a raw effect of Nazi barbarism, of the paganism or Prometheanism of history. It is inevitable that philosophy sometimes supports the victim poorly, complaining of victimary ideology or being content with a pity close to indifference, when, for example, it makes no effort to unearth its phenomenon, making of it a non-calamitous idea that falls back on the idealized mechanism of the forces of the world. To escape from the philosophical presupposition of the victim as already given and, as a result, redoubled in a juridical process of continued victimization, it must certainly "return," but as an index measuring and carrying out the decline, or under-determining the force, of the over-criminal "philosopher." The victim does not return like the criminal to the scene of the crime, but – and this is not an example but a paradigm no doubt to be transformed – returns as Christ returning to earth and into history, the scene of crimes and of salvation, a return [*une revenue*] that is rather a coming-under [*une sous-venue*]. If the criminal in the previous solution disappeared or vanished into the philosophical glory of the hero as into a tangle or a fog intended to lead its pursuers astray, the victim vanishes into itself, that is, into the Man-in-person that it is, and for its part, Man-in-person comes-under the victim.

4 To grasp the real phenomenon of the victim and understand that, according to the logic of superposition, it can be a victim offered up and resistant "at the same time" but not "simultaneously," we will begin with a formula that could be adapted from Levinas: *Man-in-person is in itself what calls for and prohibits murder, what possibilizes and impossibilizes it.* Its interpretation depends upon the response to the question: with what possibility and impossibility do we reward Man? Here, there is no question of Man, who is the minimum of

generic answer that every question must record and in relation to which every question must arise axiomatically instead of being asked anew. Indeed, we will say that *Man is the real as impossible but as possible for the world*. These are not anonymous terms, as in psychoanalysis; the terms "possible" and "impossible" and even "possibilization" and "impossibilization" belong to logic. It must be said that Man-in-person is the *possible lived experience [of] impossibility* opposed to the possibilities of the world and not to the impossibility of the lived experience, or even the virtual as under-determining condition of the actual.

We will thus break down Levinas's thesis, of which we have said that it contained perhaps a final unitary appearance. To correct this appearance, we will suppose that there is no relation of Man-in-person to the world, but that there is a relation unilaterally from the world to Man; hence, a subject is offered by the world and reduced by the Man-in-person. Beyond that, we will also suppose that there is no relation of Man to the subject, but rather of the subject to Man. Man-in-person is foreclosed to crime; this being-foreclosed, which does not render it absolutely but radically strange to the world, is also what cedes its place to the possibility of crime against subjects. Crime and resistance form a unilateral complementarity in the relations of subjects (in-the-last-instance of Man-in-person) to the world or to history.

5 Man-in-person is foreclosed to "victimological" crime. It is the resistance still without an object, a resistance to the real state of indifference, waiting for a motivating occasion. This point of indifference is the

absence of the desire to kill or to persecute as much as the desire to be killed. This is an axiom of generic neutrality as regards the victim and crime, and a way of accusing the criminal tendency of the "world": it circumscribes the properly generic sphere of the Last Instance. Obviously, we do not understand this neutrality as that of a subject or object of the act; it is the state of a glorious or arisen lived experience. That man can kill man, according to a formula more radical than that of "killing each other," is obviously an objective reality. As for Man, though, crime is a hallucination that moves the criminal and the philosopher, whereas it is the individual subject in its objective reality that is killed. As for Man, he is not a *real* victimized, he is only so through this immanental hallucination that is *the objective reality*. The possibility of or the will to crime is aimed at Man and runs aground upon his real or immanent being. On the other hand, the reality of the crime is aimed at the subject in its control. Nothing is more decisive for the subject and its struggles than this real, more-than-transcendental, hallucination through which the world becomes identified with Man and endeavors to capture him. But it is necessary to pose this indifference, an unlocalizable and untestable point, a point of non-criminality, of impossible criminality; to do otherwise is to admit – and this is total philosophical doxa – that man is a beast within humanity, a "human animal," the overly simple fusion of bestiality and humanity, with the supplementary presupposition that the animal is defined in a reflexive and vicious way by this very "human" predicate of bestiality. Man-in-person is foreclosed to the victim as a universal and global singularity, the giver of the final and most noble meaning of history (in

Christianity by the sacrifice of Christ, and in Judaism by the state of being hostage to the Other). Except for philosophy, the victim is not an exemplary man or the correlate-subject of an extraordinary event.

6 Man-in-person, foreclosed as a point of indifference to the world, is nevertheless assailed by the world as by a force of attraction for which nothing must be indifferent and which thus bears criminality with it. What is there of criminality in the form-world? We understand by hallucination the inventive confusion that the world in itself makes with that which of it is given in the immanence of Man-in-person; seeing that it is in origin immanental as regards its reality, it is not a phenomenon of psychological illusion, but an objective rather than transcendental appearance. Man-in-person is neither everything nor an example, neither an exception nor an object of election. It is necessary to state that, at the level of crime against humanity, at least at the level of what this formula targets as a symptom, no man, no people, if it is to be an example of the category of humanity, is Man-in-person.

If then the world has its reasons (to believe it is able) to persecute Man-in-person, it only kills and does not kill under and within a hallucinatory macroscopic form. In general, crime and victimization are thought as tracings of the empirical, despite this other ultimate and more utopian dimension. To hallucinate Man is to desire him, to re-present the unrepresentable, even to redouble him, to make him come out through an auto-position and make of him a being of the world; this is to transcend towards Man. As soon as philosophy thinks Man, it always kills him twice, not only in an empirico-transcendental way, but also as a metaphysical object, rational animal, and these likewise twice. This is a formal murder, but which gives to empirical slaughter its final meaning. The All is not only transcendental or empirico-transcendental, it is also an auto-encompassing All, an above-All that shrouds itself or claims to be "real" and absolute. There is thus a confirmation, a reaffirmation of the empirical murder that claims to be real, the leap into the Absolute of the All. Man is not murderable, but the form-world kills him by reformulating him as present in the world, implanted in it as subject. Completely developed philosophy no doubt contrasts killing and protecting, and gives primacy to protection, but this is but a more subtle form of hallucination.

7 Therefore, it would be necessary to distinguish in all clarity two phases of victimization, of the desire for murder. (1) The victim in a full sense is a victim in relation to the *redoubled All* of the world; it is the twofold victim, posed twice, reaffirmed, its highest concept. It is over-criminalized or over-victimized, the correlate of deployed philosophy or of the form-world, of the last or first desire to murder, a hallucinatory level of evil that precisely makes the "originary" generic resistance appear. The world is criminal as force-of-force; reaffirming itself, it is a redoubled forcing that forces man to appear, to make himself visible in the form of the world. Man is entitled to secrecy, but the world is the forced parousia of Man, who thus appears as victim. (2) In relation now to the transcendental or *simple All* that is "philosophy," the victim is trivialized in doxa and communicates directly with ethical, juridical, and

psychological concepts. It is at this level that the struggle against philosophical victimization (to which we have reduced the Greco-Judaic context) is deployed, but on the acquired basis of resistance. This is the phase of the subject that alone leads – with the means of the world – the struggle against transcendental criminality, this time the world's. The ideological theme of the victim is spontaneously contemplative or gives rise to such an attitude. But one will ask if it unleashes a struggle and a specific practice of and for victims. A good understanding of the victim's resistance means not remaining there but using the victim, this time against the encompassing All. If Man-in-person is not a victim, it is necessary that it assert itself or come-under as subject, victim of the world, which is already a form of resistance or of an a priori that manifests the world as criminal. There is a messianity of the victim that persists in the process of de-criminalization.

8 Man as such, not having acted reflexively, which is to say reacted immediately and from himself (to aggression), having thus rendered the first aggression possible, this time re-acts or defends himself by an a priori prohibition. This prohibition of killing is an a priori emitted by Man in front or in-prior-priority of the aggression that nevertheless already took place. How to resolve this paradox? If criminality is first, and relies or "counts" on real human passivity, the generic defense is prior-to-the first, and from this point of view it is then impossible to "rely on" it to not react. The real non-acting is a temptation for the world to act in a criminal way, but the same non-acting is not in itself victim; it is efficacious in a non-mechanical or non-transcendent way in that it

has already "anticipated" and foreseen aggression and posed the condition of defense. The prior-to-the-first condition, in its non-acting, is not an insufficiency, an involuntary or accepted weakness: weak force is not a lesser force against the force-of-force. This a priori of defense (the clone) has a real condition, which can use the means of aggression to defend itself, turning them against the aggressor; this is its way of organizing resistance, not exactly a "passive resistance" as much as a resistance prior-to-the-first. For the aggressor, there is resistance *at the same time* as aggression, or victim at the same time as defense, as we said. This is its illusion of simultaneity, and the paradox in all that makes it incomprehensible or vicious. There is no vicious circle as there is in philosophy, but a *single superposed power of being victim-and-resistant, divided up on occasion.* This in no way excludes in resistance the recourse to the means of the aggressor, and thus to his "help," compelled in spite of him.

9 Being-foreclosed or non-acting is deployed as acting by a clone or resistance. In this resistance, Man-in-person comes-under as messianity. The prohibition is not in itself like a law-thing absolutely affecting and subjectivating conscience; it is messianic, *that which comes as human in front of the world and not into its milieu; this is the resistance to the desire to murder.* It is neither a law nor the Law, which itself never comes immanently or only comes with a load of transcendence. The prohibition of killing has for real phenomenal content a lived experience (of) resistance to this criminal drive of the world. But this resistance is no longer a form of heroism, or rather it is a "weak heroism." The

victim is prior-to-the-first in relation to the world, and it is the victim that a priori gives form to the criminal, the force that manifests crime. It institutes a new visibility of the criminal.

Hallucinatory regarding Man, real murder thus supposes a passive resistance to the form-world. Because the Jews experienced this moment of passive resistance, but under its transcendent aspect, they made of it the whole of possible resistance. Yet it conditions the struggle against victimization. As immanent messianity, resistance unfolding a priori allows us to avoid fixing upon this moment contemplatively and demanding reparation, but inversely it avoids understanding the victim as hero and ending in an over-heroization of Man. Resistance thus appears with the victim and not after it (except as regards the occasion). Being-victim is the prior-to-the-first phenomenon of resistance and makes it understood that a struggle is possible rather than hopeless either through defeat or through an already acquired victory.

10 The victim is not the invisible Man, or does not exhaust him; the victim is the appearance or the single face, the uniface that Man tolerates as a resistant, his representative as a clone or Stranger. The victim is "less" invisible than he; the victim is what he is able to possess of the phenomenal in an essence that is radically and not absolutely invisible. The victim's weakness, its miscomprehension as soon as it is seen from the point of view of the criminal, comes from being semi-visible and semi-represented and thus susceptible to lapse sometimes towards the world, sometimes towards Man-in-person. Philosophy presents itself as a *Principle of*

Sufficient Justice, as if it sufficed to philosophize the victim in order to do it justice. *The victim conceptualized by philosophy is the victim from the point of view of the criminal, criminalized or murdered twice, reduced to a bad weakness, a lack of force; all this is begun by refusing the victim justice and reality.* But the victim is also the mid-space [*mi-lieu*] that dualizes the world as criminal. It is a backwards margin for the world; it comes as messianity for the relations of force; it stands before crime. This non-relation of the victim to crime allows for the displacement and transformation of their relation.

11 Lastly, a necessary but non-sufficient deduction of the function of the intellectual is possible. It is a matter of the generic intellectual (self) producing practically (as) a knowledge of the victim, which itself knows itself [*se sait*] victim without recognizing itself [*se connaître*] as such, or *without necessarily having the means, even if it has the capacity to do so,* of implementing the capacity of resistance it possesses. Thus it is a question of constituting the couple victim/intellectual in a single vector of resistance that holds for one and the other. This couple is complex and obscures the possibility of a triad because it is founded upon the relation of the dominant intellectual or the victimizing philosopher to the victim. This relation is transformed in the generic matrix by the revival of the victim as under-determining, from the intellectual relation of domination to the non-relation of immanent imitation or cloning, by which the intellectual comes to the aid of the victim by being made in its turn not simple or brute victim but subject-clone. The generic intellectual with his affects, such as

compassion, is drawn from the philosopher that he was, cloned from him under the condition of the victim. He is the part of the philosopher that the victim can clone. In other words, there is a single vectorial equation or a vector state for the victim and the intellectual. The intellectual passes through the two states; in general, he helps the victim acquire the power to manifest, judge, and thus "save" the criminal. But he contributes to saving himself (judging himself, condemning himself, etc.) by superposing himself on the victim and abandoning his spontaneously or "unconsciously" criminal side.

Index

Index

Index

Index

Index

Index